GCSE RELIGIOUS STUDIES FOR EDEXCEL B

Religion and Ethics

through Christianity

Gordon Reid and Sarah K Tyler

OXFORD
UNIVERSITY PRESS

Great Clarendon Street, Oxford, OX2 6DP, United Kingdom

Oxford University Press is a department of the University of Oxford. It furthers the University's objective of excellence in research, scholarship, and education by publishing worldwide. Oxford is a registered trade mark of Oxford University Press in the UK and in certain other countries

© Oxford University Press 2016

The moral rights of the authors have been asserted

First published in 2016

All rights reserved. No part of this publication may be reproduced, stored in a retrieval system, or transmitted, in any form or by any means, without the prior permission in writing of Oxford University Press, or as expressly permitted by law, by licence or under terms agreed with the appropriate reprographics rights organization. Enquiries concerning reproduction outside the scope of the above should be sent to the Rights Department, Oxford University Press, at the address above.

You must not circulate this work in any other form and you must impose this same condition on any acquirer

British Library Cataloguing in Publication Data
Data available

978-0-19-837040-6

10 9 8 7 6 5 4 3

Paper used in the production of this book is a natural, recyclable product made from wood grown in sustainable forests. The manufacturing process conforms to the environmental regulations of the country of origin.

Printed in India by Multivista Global Pvt. Ltd

Links to third party websites are provided by Oxford in good faith and for information only. Oxford disclaims any responsibility for the materials contained in any third party website referenced in this work.

endorsed for
edexcel

In order to ensure that this resource offers high-quality support for the associated Pearson qualification, it has been through a review process by the awarding body. This process confirms that this resource fully covers the teaching and learning content of the specification or part of a specification at which it is aimed. It also confirms that it demonstrates an appropriate balance between the development of subject skills, knowledge and understanding, in addition to preparation for assessment.

Endorsement does not cover any guidance on assessment activities or processes (e.g. practice questions or advice on how to answer assessment questions), included in the resource nor does it prescribe any particular approach to the teaching or delivery of a related course.

While the publishers have made every attempt to ensure that advice on the qualification and its assessment is accurate, the official specification and associated assessment guidance materials are the only authoritative source of information and should always be referred to for definitive guidance.

Pearson examiners have not contributed to any sections in this resource relevant to examination papers for which they have responsibility.

Examiners will not use endorsed resources as a source of material for any assessment set by Pearson.

Endorsement of a resource does not mean that the resource is required to achieve this Pearson qualification, nor does it mean that it is the only suitable material available to support the qualification, and any resource lists produced by the awarding body shall include this and other appropriate resources.

Thank you

From the authors:

Our special thanks to Lois and Sarah at OUP – simply brilliant!

From the publisher:

OUP wishes to thank Philip H Robinson, RE Adviser to the CES, Revd Dr Mark Griffiths, and Elisabeth Hoey for their valuable help in reviewing and contributing to this book.

Contents

Edexcel GCSE Religious Studies

This book covers all you'll need to study for Edexcel GCSE Religious Studies Paper 1B: Religion and Ethics through Christianity. Whether you're studying for the full course or the short course, this book will provide the knowledge you'll need, as well as plenty of opportunities to prepare for your GCSE examinations.

GCSE Religious Studies provides the opportunity to study a truly fascinating subject: it will help you to debate big moral issues, understand and analyse a diverse range of opinions, as well as to think for yourself about the meaning of life.

How is the specification covered?

- The Edexcel specification is split into **four sections**:
  - *Christian Beliefs*
  - *Marriage and the Family*
  - *Living the Christian Life*
  - *Matters of Life and Death*

This book has **four chapters** which match these sections. If you are taking the short course, you will only need to cover the first two sections: *Christian Beliefs*, and *Marriage and the Family*.

- Each of the four sections of the specification is split into **eight sub-sections**. These cover specific topics, like 'creation', or 'worship'. To support this, each chapter in this book is also split into the same eight sub-sections.

How to use this book

- So that you are fully prepared for your exams, you need to work through every chapter of this book (or just the first two for the short course). At the end of every topic there are exam-style questions which you should use to test your knowledge and practise your writing. Answering exam questions regularly, throughout your GCSE course, will really help you to be confident when exam time arrives.

- In the main topics there are lots of features to guide you through the material:

Specification focus provides you with the relevant description from the Edexcel specification, so that you can see exactly what the exam board expects you to know.

Support features help you to secure important knowledge, and **Stretch** features provide the opportunity for a challenge.

Build your skills are activities that focus on developing the skills you'll need for your exams, and consolidating the knowledge you'll need too.

A **compare and contrast** feature appears in 1.6 and 3.1. On these topics in your exam you may be required to compare Christian beliefs to another religion you are studying.

Exam-style questions gives two exam questions so that you can have a go at writing about the information you've studied in that topic. The letter at the start of each question tells you the question type (**a**, **b**, **c**, or **d**), and the number in brackets at the end tells you how many marks you are aiming for.

Sources of wisdom and authority will appear in boxes like this. Important, learnable phrases within a quote will often be in **bold**.

Useful terms are **orange** in the text and defined here. All of these terms are also provided in an alphabetical **glossary** at the end of the book.

Summary provides a short, bullet-pointed list of key information for ease of reference.

- At the end of every chapter there are a few pages called 'Revision and Exam practice'. These are designed to help you revise the information you have studied in that chapter, and coach you as you practise writing exam answers.

Four **exam-style questions** are provided – one for each of the question types **a**, **b**, **c**, and **d**.

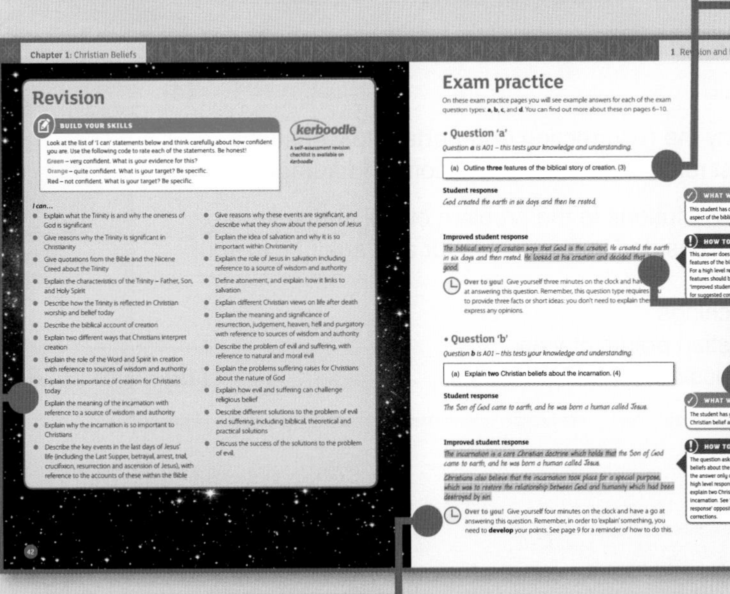

Working through this revision checklist, and following up on anything you might have missed, will help you to make sure you've revised all of the important information from the chapter.

For each exam question, a sample **student answer** is provided, followed by an **improved** version so that you can be guided through improving your own answers.

What went well lists the good things about the first student response. **How to improve** lists its weaknesses, and suggests changes that should be made. These changes are reflected in the 'improved student response'.

Over to you! suggests that you have a go at answering the question yourself under exam conditions, and provides a few final exam tips.

Exam skills: What will the exams be like?

If you are studying the full course, you will sit **two** examinations, each **1 hour and 45 minutes** long. One exam will cover the content in this book (on Christianity), and the other will cover a second faith option.

If you are studying the short course, you will sit **two** examinations, each **50 minutes** long. One exam will cover the first two chapters of content in this book (on Christianity), and the other will cover a second faith option.

You must answer all of the questions on the exam paper.

Exam structure

Because this book covers just **one** of your two exams, the following information relates to that exam. For the full course exam, there will be **four questions** to answer. For the short course exam, there will be **two questions** to answer. Each question will relate to one of the four chapters in this book:

1. **Christian Beliefs**
2. **Marriage and the Family**
3. **Living the Christian Life**
4. **Matters of Life and Death**

Short course: answer two questions on these first two topics

Full course: answer four questions, one for each of these four topics

Each question will be split into four parts: **a**, **b**, **c**, and **d**. For example, your first question on the exam (covering *1. Christian Beliefs*) could be something like this:

1 (a) Outline **three** features of the Trinity. **(3)**

(b) Explain **two** types of evil. **(4)**

(c) Explain **two** reasons why the resurrection is important to Christians. In your answer you must refer to a source of wisdom and authority. **(5)**

(d) "Christianity provides no solutions to the problem of evil and suffering." Evaluate this statement considering arguments for and against. In your response you should:

- refer to Christian teachings
- refer to different Christian points of view
- reach a justified conclusion. **(15)**

The 'a' question

The 'a' question will always start with the words 'Outline **three**...' or 'State **three**', and the maximum number of marks awarded will be three marks. For example:

1 (a)	Outline **three** features of the Trinity.	**(3)**

The 'b' question

The 'b' question will always start with the words 'Explain **two**...' or 'Describe **two**...', and the maximum number of marks awarded will be four marks. For example:

(b)	Explain **two** types of evil.	**(4)**

The 'c' question

The 'c' question will always start with the words 'Explain **two**...', and will ask you to refer to a source of wisdom and authority. The maximum number of marks awarded will be five marks. For example:

(c)	Explain **two** reasons why the resurrection is important to Christians. In your answer you must refer to a source of wisdom and authority.	**(5)**

The 'd' question

The 'd' question will always start with a statement of opinion that you are asked to evaluate. These questions will sometimes be out of 12 marks, and sometimes be out of 15 marks (see page 11, 'Written communication', to find out why!). For example:

(d) "Christianity provides no solutions to the problem of evil and suffering."
Evaluate this statement considering arguments for and against. In your response you should:
- refer to Christian teachings
- refer to different Christian points of view
- reach a justified conclusion. **(15)**

Know your question types!

...that way, nothing in your exam will take you by surprise!

Exam skills: How will the exams be marked?

When you're revising and practising using exam questions, it will really help you to understand how you'll be marked. If you know what the examiners are looking for, then you're more likely to do well!

Assessment Objectives

Examiners will mark your work using two Assessment Objectives: Assessment Objective 1 (AO1), and Assessment Objective 2 (AO2). The two Assessment Objectives are described in the table below.

	Students must:	Weighting
AO1	Demonstrate knowledge and understanding of religion and belief, including: • beliefs, practices and sources of authority • influence on individuals, communities and societies • similarities and differences within and/or between religions and beliefs.	50%
AO2	Analyse and evaluate aspects of religion and belief, including their significance and influence.	50%

You need to remember that 50% of the marks available in your exam will be awarded for demonstrating **knowledge and understanding of religion and belief** (AO1), and 50% of the marks available will be awarded for **analysing and evaluating aspects of religion and belief** (AO2).

Marking the 'a' question

'Outline/State' questions are assessed using Assessment Objective 1 (knowledge) only. These questions require you to provide three facts or short ideas: **you don't need to explain them or express any opinions**. For example, in answer to the question 'Outline **three** features of the Trinity', your three responses could be:

1. There is one God in three persons (1)
2. Each person is fully God (1)
3. Each person is different from the other persons (1)

For each response, you would receive 1 mark. You're not expected to spend time explaining what the Trinity is: the question only asks you to give three features.

Marking the 'b' question

Like the 'a' question, 'b' questions are assessed using Assessment Objective 1 (knowledge) only. However, 'b' questions start with 'Explain' or 'Describe', which means you will need to show **development** of ideas. For example, if the question is 'Explain **two** types of evil' you might think you just need to state the two types, but this means you can only be awarded **a maximum of two marks**:

Type 1: One type of evil is called natural evil (1)

Type 2: Another type of evil is called moral evil (1)

The types given above are correct, but the student would only score 2 marks out of 4. In order to fully **explain** these reasons, you need to show some **development**. For example:

Type 1: One type of evil is called natural evil (1), **which means evil caused by nature, e.g. earthquakes (1)**

Type 2: Another type of evil is called moral evil (1), **which means evil caused by humans, e.g. murder (1)**

Each of the above points are now developed, and would receive 2 marks each, totalling **4 marks**.

CONNECTIVES

A **connective** helps you to develop your basic answer. There are lots of different types of connective (therefore/because/and/consequently/a result of this is/this means that). However, take care not to simply repeat the question and then use a connective, as that is not a developed answer and is only worth one mark. For example, 'Christians believe in two types of evil, **and** one of these is called natural evil' would only receive one mark despite the use of a connective.

Marking the 'c' question

Like the 'a' and 'b' questions, 'c' questions are assessed using Assessment Objective 1 (knowledge) only. 'C' questions are very similar to 'b' questions (they begin with 'Explain **two**' and require two developed points), but they have one crucial difference. For an extra mark, you are expected to include a reference to a **source of wisdom and authority**, which could be a quotation from/reference to the Bible or another important source within Christianity. For example, here's a student answer to a five-mark question:

(c) Explain **two** reasons why the resurrection is important to Christians. In your answer you must refer to a source of wisdom and authority. **(5)**

Christians believe that Jesus' resurrection allows their sins to be forgiven **(1)**. Therefore, they can have a true relationship with God again **(1)**. If Christians repent, they will be forgiven (Luke 24: 47) **(1)**.

Jesus' resurrection means that death is not the end **(1)**; this means that he showed that death could be overcome and he paved the way for Christians to be with God **(1)**.

You need to write **two** developed points, one of which needs to be supported by a source of wisdom and authority. Setting out your writing in two paragraphs makes it clear that it is two developed points. You could directly quote a source, or you could just include the reference (as in the above student answer).

Marking the 'd' question

The 'd' question is marked using AO2 (analysis/evaluation). These questions specifically ask you to evaluate a statement. Evaluating a statement means that you are weighing up how good or true it is. The best way to evaluate something is to consider different opinions on the matter – and this is exactly what the question asks you to do. When you are planning your answer, you need to remember to do the following:

- Refer to Christian teachings – for instance core beliefs and important sources of wisdom and authority
- Ensure that different viewpoints are included either from within Christianity or non-religious views, and ensure that relevant ethical or philosophical arguments are referred to (the question will make it clear which of these will be required in your answer)
- Ensure that you include a justified conclusion – in other words, your final decision on the matter having considered different viewpoints.

If you don't refer to different viewpoints, **you cannot get more than half of the marks**.

The examiner will mark your answer using a **mark scheme**, similar to the one below.

Level	Descriptor
Level 1 (1–3 marks)	• Basic information or reasons about the issue are identified and can be explained by some religious or moral understanding. • Opinions are given but not fully explained.
Level 2 (4–6 marks)	• Some information or reasons about the issue are loosely identified and can be explained by limited religious or moral understanding. • Opinions are given which attempt to support the issue but are not fully explained or justified.
Level 3 (7–9 marks)	• Information given clearly describes religious information/issues, leading to coherent and logical chains of reasoning **that consider different viewpoints**. These are supported by an accurate understanding of religion and belief. • The answer contains coherent and reasoned judgements of many, but not all, of the elements in the question. Judgements are supported by a good understanding of evidence, leading to a partially justified conclusion.
Level 4 (10–12 marks)	• The response critically deconstructs religious information/issues, leading to coherent and logical chains of reasoning **that consider different viewpoints.** These are supported by a sustained, accurate and thorough understanding of religion and belief. • The answer contains coherent and reasoned judgements of the full range of elements in the question. Judgements are fully supported by the comprehensive use of evidence, leading to a fully justified conclusion.

ARE YOU READY?

Written communication

Some of the marks in your exam will be awarded purely for the quality of your 'written communication'. Written communication includes your use of correct **spelling, punctuation and grammar**, as well as the use of **specialist terminology**.

These marks will be awarded in questions **1(d)** and **3(d)**: these are the long essay questions on topics 1 and 3 (*Christian Beliefs* and *Living the Christian Life*). Whereas 'd' questions in topics 2 and 4 are out of 12 marks, these will be out of **15 marks**, and the extra 3 marks in each question are awarded solely for your written communication. You'll know which questions these are in the exam because they will be shown with an asterisk (*) and have a really clear instruction above them:

In this question, 3 of the marks awarded will be for your spelling, punctuation and grammar and your use of specialist terminology.

*(d) "Christianity provides no solutions to the problem of evil and suffering."

Evaluate this statement considering arguments for and against. In your response you should:
- refer to Christian teachings
- refer to different Christian points of view
- reach a justified conclusion. **(15)**

In these questions:
- 0 marks are awarded if there are considerable errors or irrelevant information
- 1 mark is awarded for reasonable accuracy and limited use of religious terms
- 2 marks are awarded for considerable accuracy and a good number of specialist terms
- 3 marks are awarded for consistent accuracy and a wide range of specialist terms.

Good written communication is always important, but you will only receive marks for it in questions **1(d)** and **3(d)**. Therefore, you should allow yourself time in your exam to check these two essays carefully and amend any errors.

Introduction to Christianity

What is Christianity?

Christianity is the main religious tradition in Great Britain. Other religious traditions include Islam, Buddhism, Judaism, Hinduism and Sikhism.

Central to Christianity is a man named Jesus, whose existence in first-century Palestine has been recorded by early Roman and Jewish scholars. The life and impact of Jesus is described in the New Testament of the Bible – the Christian holy book – including the claim that Jesus is the Son of God, and accounts of the work of his followers, the early Christians.

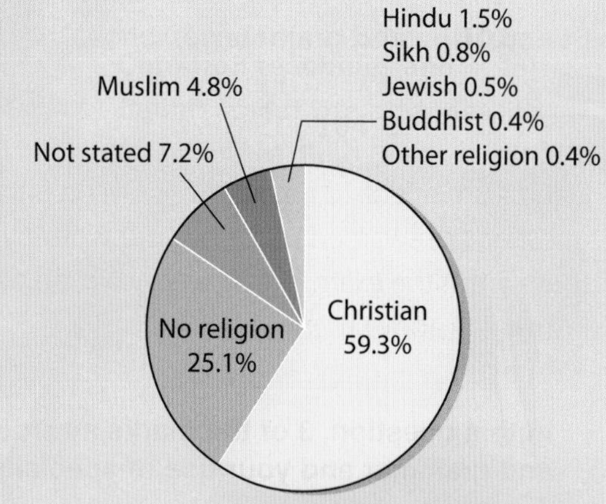

The 2011 England and Wales census asked people, 'What is your religion?'. This pie chart shows how people responded.

What do Christians believe?

Christians believe in one God in three persons: God the Father, God the Son (who came to earth as Jesus) and God the Holy Spirit (see 1.1). Christians believe that God loves them, and wants to have a relationship with them. They believe that, because of this love, he sent Jesus to live amongst them, to die on a cross and be raised to life three days later. They believe he did this to free humanity from sin, and make it possible for them to spend eternity with God in heaven (see 1.3–1.5).

While he was on earth, Jesus chose twelve specific followers, who are known within Christianity as the apostles, or disciples. He also had many other followers, however, including women and children. According to the Bible, after his death and resurrection Jesus' followers gathered in Jerusalem, and the number of followers grew quickly from hundreds to thousands as the apostles began to teach about Jesus and the things they had experienced.

What are the different groups within Christianity?

Today, Christianity has followers all over the world. The word 'denomination' is used to describe a particular group within Christianity. There are many different denominations which you will learn about in this book.

The Catholic Church and the Orthodox Church

The Catholic Church was the only Christian Church until 1054CE. Around 1054CE, a new denomination was formed, one that we now refer to as the Orthodox Church. There were many reasons why this split occurred, but a key reason was that the Orthodox Church did not believe the Pope (the leader of the Catholic Church) should have ultimate authority.

The Protestant denominations

In 1517, Martin Luther, a Catholic priest, challenged a range of Catholic practices. His followers were called 'Lutherans', and shortly after, the Lutheran Church was formed. It was, in effect, the first of the Protestant denominations, which developed as a 'protest' against the practices of the Catholic Church.

Since that time, a number of Protestant denominations have formed, for example:

- The Church of England (sometimes called the Anglican Church)
- The Baptist Church
- The Methodist Church
- The Salvation Army
- Pentecostal denominations.

New denominations continue to form today, and usually come out of existing denominations. They are formed because of differences over two main factors:

1. Governance (the way the denomination is structured)
2. Theology (what the denomination believes).

Today, it is very important to understand that there is a lot of overlap among denominations, particularly the larger denominations. For example, charismatic worship (traditionally associated with the Pentecostal church) can be found in Anglican and Catholic churches (see 3.1). Many churches also work together, which is called ecumenism (see 3.7).

Christians in Great Britain today

From a dozen people in Jerusalem in the first century, Christianity now has more than 2.4 billion believers all over the world. In Great Britain, Christianity is still the main religious tradition, despite a growing number of people who do not identify with any particular religion.

The study of Christianity will enable you to develop a greater understanding of the practice of Christianity in Great Britain and the wider world, and to consider the values held by Christians. This book provides you with opportunities to make your own observations, raise questions, and draw personal conclusions about various teachings, beliefs and important issues.

Chapter 1: Christian Beliefs

Chapter contents	Specification mapping	Page
Chapter 1: Christian Beliefs	Section 1: Christian Beliefs	14
1.1 The Trinity	1.1 The Trinity: the nature and significance of the Trinity as expressed in the Nicene Creed; the nature and significance of the oneness of God; the nature and significance of each of the Persons individually: including reference to Matthew 3: 13–17; how this is reflected in Christian worship and belief today.	16
1.2 Creation	1.2 The creation of the universe and of humanity: the biblical account of creation and divergent ways in which it may be understood by Christians, including as literal and metaphorical; the role of the Word and Spirit in creation including John 1: 1–18 and Genesis 1–3; the importance of creation for Christians today.	20
1.3 The incarnation	1.3 The incarnation: the nature and importance of the person of Jesus Christ as the incarnate Son of God; the biblical basis of this teaching, including John 1: 1–18 and 1 Timothy 3: 16 and its significance for Christians today.	24
1.4 The last days of Jesus' life	1.4 The last days of Jesus' life: the Last Supper, betrayal, arrest, trial, crucifixion, resurrection and ascension of Jesus; the accounts of these within the Bible, including Luke 22–24 and the significance of these events to understanding the person of Jesus Christ.	26
1.5 Salvation	1.5 The nature and significance of salvation and the role of Christ within salvation: law, sin, grace and Spirit, the role of Christ in salvation including John 3: 10–21 and Acts 4: 8–12; the nature and significance of atonement within Christianity and its link to salvation.	30
1.6 Christian eschatology **This topic should be compared with another religion you have studied.*	1.6 Christian eschatology: divergent Christian teachings about life after death, including the nature and significance of resurrection, judgement, heaven, and hell and purgatory, with reference to the 39 Articles of Religion and Catholic teachings; how beliefs about life after death are shown in the Bible, including reference to 2 Corinthians 5: 1–10 and divergent understandings as to why they are important for Christians today.	33
1.7 The problem of evil	1.7 The problem of evil/suffering and a loving and righteous God: the problems it raises for Christians about the nature of God, including reference to omnipotence and benevolence, including Psalm 103; how the problem may cause believers to question their faith or the existence of God; the nature and examples of natural suffering, moral suffering.	36
1.8 Divergent solutions to the problem of evil	1.8 Divergent solutions offered to the problem of evil/suffering and a loving and righteous God: biblical, theoretical and practical, including reference to Psalm 119, Job, free will, vale of soul-making, prayer, and charity; the success of solutions to the problem.	38
Revision and Exam practice	**Revision checklist, exam questions, sample answers and guidance**	42

1.1 The Trinity

SPECIFICATION FOCUS

The Trinity: the nature and significance of the Trinity as expressed in the Nicene Creed; the nature and significance of the oneness of God; the nature and significance of each of the Persons individually: including reference to Matthew 3: 13–17; how this is reflected in Christian worship and belief today.

What is the Trinity?

The **Trinity** is unique to Christianity. It is the belief that there is only one God, but that he exists in three 'persons':

- God the Father
- God the Son
- God the Holy Spirit (sometimes called the Holy Ghost).

Each of these three persons is fully God, but they are not *three* Gods – they are *one* God.

The Nicene Creed

The Nicene Creed is a statement of belief that many Christians recite in church. It says of the Trinity:

> 'We believe in one God, the Father, the Almighty, maker of heaven and earth [...] We believe in one Lord, **Jesus Christ**, the only Son of God, eternally **begotten** of the Father [...] We believe in the **Holy Spirit**, the giver of life, who proceeds from the Father and the Son.'

SUPPORT

This quotation contains some difficult ideas:

- **'eternally begotten'** means that the Son of God has always existed, and is in a relationship as Son of the Father.
- **'proceeds from the Father'** means the Holy Spirit comes directly (proceeds) from God. Like the Son of God, the Holy Spirit is not *made by* God but *is* God.

The Nicene Creed reveals the following about the nature of the Trinity:

- **God the Father** is the creator of the universe and is the 'Almighty' (having complete power).
- **God the Son** is Jesus Christ who is 'Lord' and the Son of the Father.
- **God the Holy Spirit** comes from the Father and the Son. Christians believe the Holy Spirit is the 'giver of life', meaning he is spiritually active in the world, he helps them to know God and worship him, and he equips and empowers believers.

USEFUL TERMS

Begotten: born of

Holy Spirit: the Spirit of God, who gives the power to understand and worship

Jesus Christ: the Son of God, who came into the world as a human being

Trinity: God as one being, in three persons

What is the 'oneness' of God?

The Trinity can be a difficult idea to understand. For example, how can God be 'one' and 'three' at the same time? Think of the Trinity like diagram **A**. There is one God. There are three different persons, each of whom is different from the other two but each of whom is fully God. This is the special 'oneness' of God.

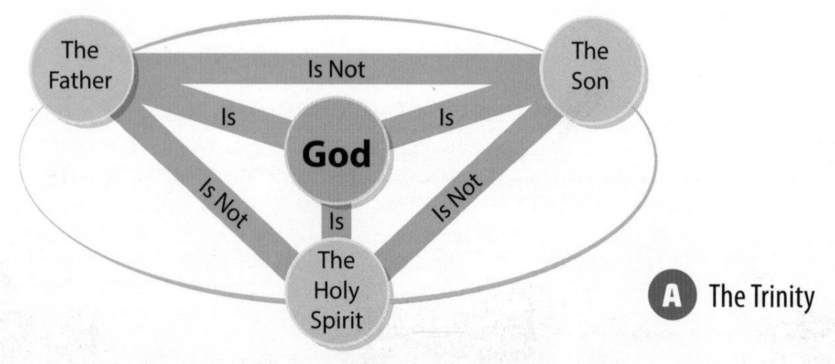

A The Trinity

The persons of the Trinity

The word 'Trinity' does not appear in the Bible. However, there is one event, described in the Gospel of Matthew, where the persons of the Trinity do all appear together. This is when Jesus is baptised before beginning his ministry in the world:

> As soon as **Jesus** was baptised, he went up out of the water. At that moment heaven was opened, and he saw **the Spirit of God** descending like a dove and alighting on him. And a **voice from heaven** said, "This is my Son, whom I love; with him I am well pleased."
> *(Matthew 3: 16–17)*

This is important because it shows the Trinity working together as one – Jesus is baptised to begin his ministry, the Father speaks his approval, and the Holy Spirit, with the power of the Father, enables Jesus to begin his work.

B *The Baptism of Christ*, a painting by Paolo Veronese (c.1580CE–1588CE)

STRETCH

Look at this painting and the corresponding story in the Bible (*Matthew 3: 13–17*). Can you find three different symbolic ideas? Why do you think these ideas are important for Christians?

The Bible highlights the importance of each person of the Trinity and how they can be understood and worshipped by Christians today.

> Therefore go and make disciples of all nations, baptising them in the name of the Father and of the Son and of the Holy Spirit.
> *(Matthew 28: 19)*

> The grace of our Lord Jesus Christ, and the love of God, and the fellowship of the Holy Spirit be with you.
> *(2 Corinthians 13: 14)*

How is the Trinity reflected in worship and belief today?

Christians use the Trinity as the guide for worship and belief. Christians believe that the Trinity displays God's loving nature, which impacts on their worship.

- **God the Father:** Christians believe that God the Father, as the creator, cares for all that he has made. They pray to him in the knowledge that he cares about them and is powerful, like Jesus did in the Lord's Prayer: 'This, then, is how you should pray: "Our Father in heaven, hallowed be your name …"' *(Matthew 6: 9)*.
- **God the Son:** Christians believe that, around 5BCE, God the Son became a human being (see 1.3), and he was given the name Jesus. Christians believe Jesus is their saviour, friend and role-model. They follow the example set by Jesus, who came into the world to teach people how to live lives of goodness, love and faith. A core belief about Jesus is that he died to take the punishment for the sins of **humanity** (see 1.4–1.5). Worship is therefore often happy and joyful, as Christians express their thanks to God for forgiving their sins and to Jesus for the sacrifice he made.
- **God the Holy Spirit:** Christians believe that the Holy Spirit is their comforter and guide. They believe that the Holy Spirit lives in their hearts and not only enables them to lead good lives and make the right moral choices, but also helps them to praise and worship God. **Charismatic** churches, such as the Pentecostal Church and an increasing number of Anglican churches, will ask the Holy Spirit to enable them to worship using **spiritual gifts**. These church services are often less formal and involve dancing and creative expression.

USEFUL TERMS

Charismatic: a power given by God, e.g. inspired teaching

Humanity: all human beings

Spiritual gifts: gifts given by God to believers, e.g. speaking in 'tongues', a special language

C A church meeting that involves charismatic worship. Can you identify any special features of this kind of worship?

Christians believe that the Trinity is a model of mutual love and perfect unity. It helps Christians to understand more about relationships because the Trinity is very similar to the way they live. They are not alone, they have families and friends who they can talk to, enjoy time with, and often love. In the same way, Christians believe the Trinity is a loving relationship with each of the three persons relating to the others – just like a family. This 'oneness' is reflected in Christian songs and hymns:

> 'Shine, Jesus, shine, fill this land with the Father's glory. Blaze, Spirit, blaze, set our hearts on fire.'
> *'Shine, Jesus, Shine', by Graham Kendrick*

> 'Holy, holy, holy, Lord God Almighty [...] God in three persons, blessed Trinity!'
> *'Holy, Holy, Holy', by Reginald Heber*

Christians are baptised 'in the name of the Father and of the Son and of the Holy Spirit' (*Matthew 28: 19*) (see 3.2) and sometimes the sign of the cross is made with a hand gesture in three movements, reflecting the Trinity.

BUILD YOUR SKILLS

1. In pairs, write down in your own words how you would describe the Trinity. As you do so, consider the following aspects:
   - How can God be 'one' and 'three' at the same time?
   - How are the three persons different from each other?
   - Do you think the idea of the Trinity makes God easier or harder to understand? Why?
2. a. What are the reasons why Christians feel that they should believe in the Trinity?
   b. How does the idea of the Trinity help Christians?
3. Look at image **D**. How would the Holy Spirit enable Christians to respond in this situation?

EXAM-STYLE QUESTIONS

b. Explain **two** Christian beliefs about the Trinity. (4)
c. Explain **two** reasons why the concept of the Trinity is important for Christians. In your answer you must refer to a source of wisdom and authority. (5)

SUMMARY

- Christians believe in the concept of the Trinity. God is one, God is in three persons (Father, Son and Holy Spirit), and each person is fully God.
- In the Bible, all three persons were present at the baptism of Jesus (*Matthew 3: 13–17*).
- Christians worship God the Father and Jesus Christ in a formal way or in private, and many believe that the Holy Spirit helps them to worship in the most fulfilling way.

D

1.2 Creation

SPECIFICATION FOCUS

The creation of the universe and of humanity: the biblical account of creation and divergent ways in which it may be understood by Christians, including as literal and metaphorical; the role of the Word and Spirit in creation including John 1: 1–18 and Genesis 1–3; the importance of creation for Christians today.

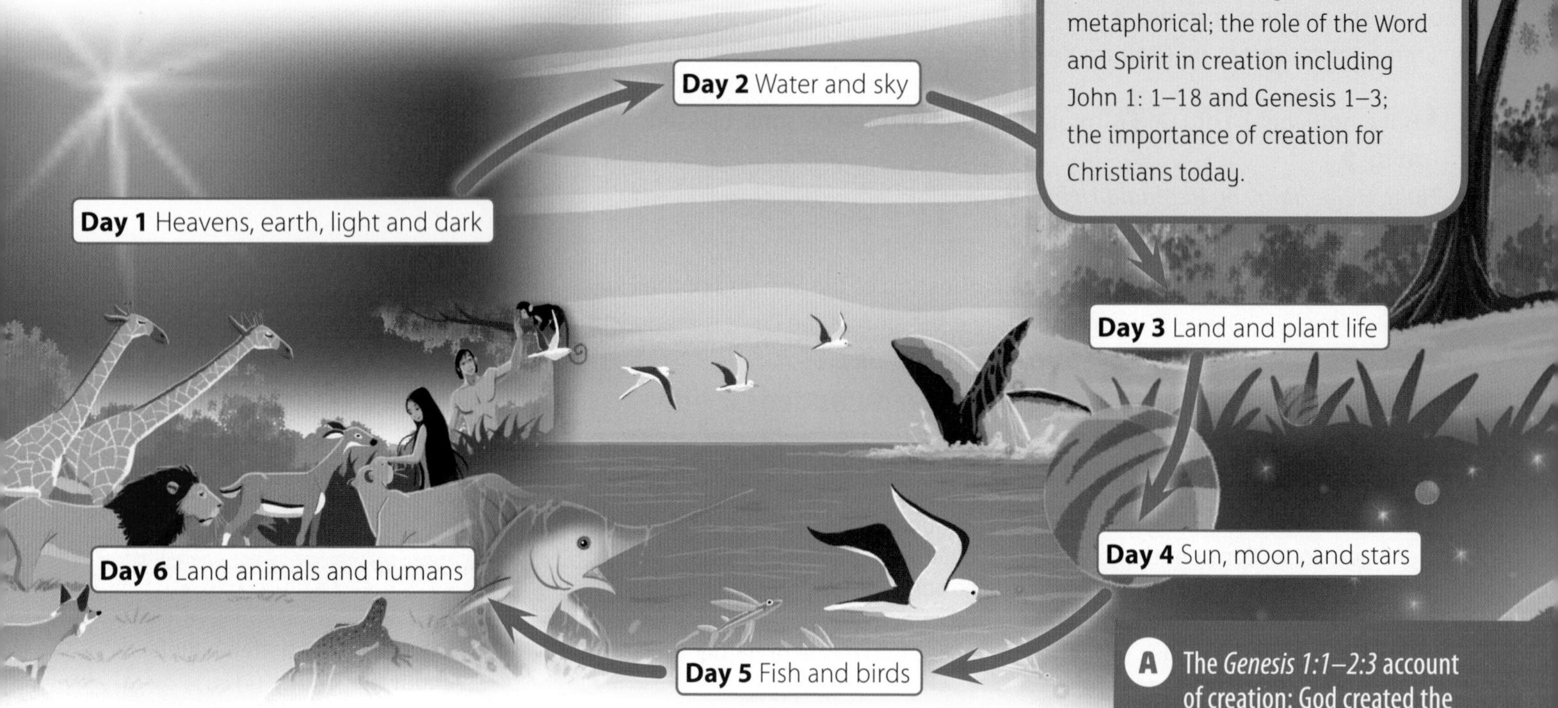

What is the biblical account of creation?

There are two accounts of creation in Genesis, the first book of the Bible. The first, in *Genesis 1:1–2:3*, contains the story of the creation of the earth by God in six days. God speaks and things happen:

A The *Genesis 1:1–2:3* account of creation: God created the earth in six days and rested on the seventh day

The second account, in *Genesis 2:4–3:23*, is different because it concentrates on the development of humans:

1. ‘Then **the Lord God formed a man** from the dust of the ground and breathed into his nostrils the breath of life, and the man became a living being.’ *(Genesis 2: 7)*

2. ‘The Lord God took the man and placed him in **the Garden of Eden** to work it and take care of it.’ *(Genesis 2: 15)*

3. ‘And the Lord God commanded the man, “You are free to eat from any tree in the garden; but **you must not eat from the tree of the knowledge of good and evil**, for when you eat from it you will certainly die.”’ *(Genesis 2: 16–17)*

4. ‘Then **the Lord God made a woman** from the rib he had taken out of the man...’ *(Genesis 2: 22)*

5. ‘When the woman saw that the fruit of the tree was good [...] **she took some and ate it. She also gave some to her husband...**’ *(Genesis 3: 6–7)*

6. ‘So the Lord God banished him from the Garden of Eden...’ *(Genesis 3: 23)*

How can the biblical account of creation be understood in different ways?

There are differing views on exactly what the Bible means in the accounts of creation:

- **The metaphorical view:** Many Christians believe this account is a metaphor, and is not literally true. They would argue that it is a story to help people to understand that God is the creator of all things.
- **The literal view:** Others believe that the Bible account is literally true and God created the world exactly as the Bible says. This is called **creationism**. Creationists believe that the Bible is the sacred word of God and believe that it should be interpreted literally where possible. Young Earth Creationists believe that the world was made in six days approximately 10,000 years ago.

USEFUL TERMS

Creationism: the belief that the world was created in a literal six days and that Genesis is a scientific/historical account of the beginning of the world

What is the role of the Word and Spirit?

The Bible teaches that God the Father, Son and Holy Spirit – the Trinity – were all involved in the act of creation.

The Word

In the New Testament, the Gospel of John says:

> '**In the beginning was the Word**, and the Word was with God, and the Word was God.'
> *(John 1:1)*
>
> '**Through him** [the Word] **all things were made** [...] In him was life...'
> *(John 1: 3–4)*

STRETCH

Read the full quotation in *John 1: 1–18*. Can you explain how this passage links to the ideas of **incarnation** and **salvation**? (See 1.3 and 1.5.)

But who is the 'Word'? The answer is Jesus, because the Gospel goes on to say, 'The Word became flesh and made his dwelling among us…' (*John 1: 14*). So Christians believe that God the Son (Jesus) was with God the Father at the start, acting in the creation. They believe he is the source of life.

The Book of Genesis also says that God created not by using his hands, but by speaking: 'God said…' (*Genesis 1: 3*). Of course, what he speaks are words – hence Jesus is 'the Word'. As it says in the Book of Psalms, 'By the word of the Lord were the heavens made…' (*Psalm 33: 6*).

The Spirit

In the Book of Genesis it says that during the act of creation the 'Spirit of God was hovering over the waters' (*Genesis 1: 2*). This image describes the Holy Spirit as present in creation to protect what has, and will be, created. The Spirit (Hebrew: 'breath') of God guards creation.

Why is creation important for Christians today?

The relationship between humans and their creator

The Bible says that man and woman were created in the image of God. Christians therefore believe that human beings are important to God, as he expressed something of himself in creating them.

- At the start, when God creates man and woman (Adam and Eve), they walk and talk with God in a relationship of love and devotion. God said, 'I give you every seed-bearing plant [...] and every tree' (*Genesis 1: 29*).
- God gave Adam and Eve **free will**, but they chose to disobey God by eating from the forbidden tree. The relationship of mutual love and trust between God and humanity was broken.
- God therefore sent Adam and Eve out of the Garden of Eden and ordered them to work the ground: 'By the sweat of your brow you will eat your food [...] for dust you are and to dust you will return' (*Genesis 3: 19*).
- Today, Christians believe that they have a personal and loving relationship with God and that they can pray to God for guidance. They believe that God has given humanity the opportunity to care for creation, with God's guidance and help.

USEFUL TERMS

Conservation: protecting something from being damaged or destroyed

Environment: the surroundings in which plants and animals live and on which they depend for life

Free will: having the freedom to choose what to do

Stewardship: looking after something so it can be passed on to the next generation

The relationship between humans and the rest of creation

Christians believe that:

- God gave humans the responsibility to look after the world as his 'stewards' (*Genesis 1: 26*). This means that they are to have authority over the animals, plants and other resources.
- God blessed humans and said, 'Be fruitful and increase in number; fill the earth and subdue it. Rule over the fish in the sea and the birds in the sky and over every living creature that moves on the ground.' (*Genesis 1: 28*).
- They should care for the environment so that the world can be passed on to future generations as a better place than when they found it. This is called **stewardship**.

STRETCH

Interestingly, at the time of Jesus, the people of Israel would celebrate a 'Year of Jubilee', when no crops were planted, to give the land a well-earned rest: 'The fiftieth year shall be a jubilee for you; do not sow and do not reap' (*Leviticus 25: 11*). Is this a good idea? Why/why not?

Christians believe humans should:

- treat animals and the land kindly
- leave the world better than they found it
- share things fairly
- be judged by God on their actions.

This means humans should take on certain duties:

- reduction of pollution
- **conservation** of resources
- sharing with the poor
- conservation of the **environment**.

B

BUILD YOUR SKILLS

1 Copy and complete the following table for the main ideas about creation given in this unit. Three ideas have been suggested for you. SUPPORT

Term/idea	What does it mean?	Why is it important for Christians?
Creation		
Stewardship		
Made in the image of God		

2 Which aspects of the biblical account of creation are **a** most convincing and **b** least convincing? Why?

3 Is God's punishment of Adam and Eve fair and just? Why/why not?

4 Look at this car used by campaigners, in image **C**.
  a What is the message being conveyed? Is it pro-creationist or anti-creationist?
  b Make a list of arguments that support creationism and a list of arguments against. Which are the most convincing arguments, and why?

5 What comes first, stopping pollution or fulfilling human needs? For example, is it right to shut down a polluting factory if it means 1000 people will lose their jobs? STRETCH

SUMMARY

- There are two accounts of how God created the world and humanity in the Book of Genesis, and there is another account in *John 1: 1–18*.
- Some Christians believe these accounts are literally true, whilst others think they are metaphorical.
- Christians believe that God has made them stewards, with a duty to care for the world and its resources.

EXAM-STYLE QUESTIONS

a Outline **three** Christian beliefs about creation. (3)

d 'A Christian should believe the world was made in seven days.' Evaluate this statement considering arguments for and against. In your response you should:
- refer to Christian teachings
- refer to different Christian points of view
- reach a justified conclusion. (15)

1.3 The incarnation

What is the incarnation?

Christians believe that Jesus Christ is the Son of God, who came down to earth to live as a man from around 5BCE to around 33CE. This is called the **incarnation**. You will be learning about the life and significance of Jesus in 1.3–1.5.

A A still image from the 1977 film *Jesus of Nazareth*. You will learn about the important ideas given on this image in 1.3–1.5.

How is the incarnation shown in the Bible?

For Christians, God the Son, the second person of the Trinity, became a human being in Jesus of Nazareth. The Bible describes the incarnation in this way:

> ‘The virgin will conceive and give birth to a son, and **they will call him Immanuel.**’
> *(Matthew 1: 23)*

> ‘The Word became flesh and made his dwelling among us.’
> *(John 1: 14)*

The Bible teaches that God the Son came into the world to live among people, show them what God was like and enable them to have a relationship with him.

SPECIFICATION FOCUS

The incarnation: the nature and importance of the person of Jesus Christ as the incarnate Son of God; the biblical basis of this teaching, including John 1: 1–18 and 1 Timothy 3: 16 and its significance for Christians today.

USEFUL TERMS

Incarnation: to take on flesh; God becomes a human being

SUPPORT

The word **incarnation** means ‘to take on flesh’: God takes on a physical human form in order to be more accessible to humanity.

Immanuel means ‘God with us’.

The Bible also describes the incarnation as a great mystery, because there are aspects of it that are amazing and beyond human understanding:

> 'Beyond all question, **the mystery from which true godliness springs is great**: He appeared in the flesh, was vindicated by the Spirit, was seen by angels, was preached among the nations, was believed on in the world, was taken up in glory.'
> *(1 Timothy 3: 16)*

STRETCH

What aspects of the incarnation are mysterious and why? Refer to this quotation from *1 Timothy* in your answer.

Vindicated means proven to be true or genuine.

What is the importance of the incarnation for Christians today?

- Christians believe that Jesus is God incarnate. They believe Jesus came into the world to enable the relationship between God and humanity to be restored (see 1.2). The incarnation is therefore important for Christians because it allows them to have a relationship with God.
- Christians believe that the incarnation shows that God loves the world and the people in it. This is what they celebrate during Christmas (see 3.5). Christians celebrate the incarnation on Christmas Day by singing Christmas carols and remembering the story of the birth of Jesus.
- Christians believe that, as a human, Jesus could understand humanity and its problems, and identify with their suffering.

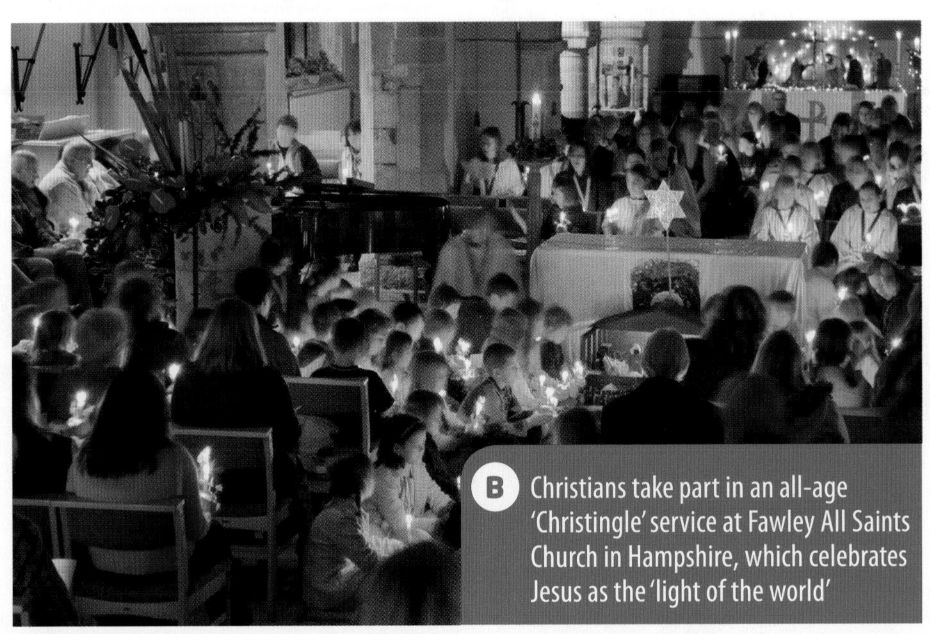

B Christians take part in an all-age 'Christingle' service at Fawley All Saints Church in Hampshire, which celebrates Jesus as the 'light of the world'

BUILD YOUR SKILLS

1 a With a partner or in a small group, write down a list of reasons why the incarnation might be true, and a list for why it might be false.
  b Which are the strongest reasons and why?

2 Why is the incarnation important for Christians? Explain two reasons in your own words. Refer to a source of wisdom and authority.

SUMMARY

- Christians believe that God came into the world as Jesus, a man. This is called the incarnation.
- The purpose of the incarnation was to enable human beings to have a relationship with God.

EXAM-STYLE QUESTIONS

a Outline **three** Christian beliefs about Jesus. (3)

c Explain **two** Christian beliefs about the incarnation of Jesus. In your answer you must refer to a source of wisdom and authority. (5)

1.4 The last days of Jesus' life

SPECIFICATION FOCUS

The last days of Jesus' life: the Last Supper, betrayal, arrest, trial, crucifixion, resurrection and ascension of Jesus; the accounts of these within the Bible, including Luke 22–24 and the significance of these events to understanding the person of Jesus Christ.

What happened in the last days of Jesus' life and why are these events important?

The Last Supper and betrayal

The evening before he died, Jesus and his disciples had a meal together, which Christians call the Last Supper. At the meal, Jesus spoke about his forthcoming death. He tried to prepare the disciples for the future by teaching them to serve one another *(Luke 22: 26–27)*. He explained that after he was gone he would send the Holy Spirit to 'teach you all things and remind you of everything I have said to you' (*John 14: 26*).

Jesus also gave the disciples bread to eat and wine to drink. He said that they are his 'body' and his 'blood'. They represented his sacrifice – 'This is my body given for you' *(Luke 22: 19)* (see 3.2).

Jesus also knew that one of the disciples would betray him, having him arrested by the Jewish authorities. He said to the disciples: 'the hand of him who is going to betray me is with mine on the table. […] But woe to that man who betrays [me]' *(Luke 22: 21–22)*. It was Judas Iscariot who betrayed him.

For Christians, these events highlight that Jesus' teachings had begun to come true – he knew what was going to happen. Christians remember the Last Supper when they take part in the Eucharist (see 3.2).

STRETCH

Read the full story in *Luke 22: 7–38*. What can Christians learn about the person of Jesus from this passage?

A *The Sacrament of the Last Supper* by Salvador Dalí (1955)

Jesus' betrayal, arrest, and trial

Jesus and the disciples planned to spend the night in a garden called Gethsemane. In the middle of the night, Judas Iscariot brought an armed crowd to take Jesus away. Judas identified Jesus to the authorities by kissing him *(Luke 22: 47–48)*.

Jesus was taken before the Jewish High Council, called the Sanhedrin. They found Jesus guilty of blasphemy for claiming to be the Son of God. They believed that this was a great crime which should be punished by death.

Blasphemy means insulting or showing a lack of respect for God.

After this, the Jewish leaders took Jesus to the Roman governor, Pontius Pilate, who sentenced Jesus to death even though Pilate thought he was innocent: "'Why? What crime has this man committed? I have found in him no grounds for the death penalty'" *(Luke 23: 22)*.

The crucifixion

Jesus was put to death by **crucifixion**, which means being nailed to a cross and left to die. He was crucified between two criminals. The sky went dark from midday until around 3pm, when he died.

USEFUL TERMS

Crucifixion: being nailed to a cross and left to die

Sin: anything that prevents a relationship with God, either because the person does something they shouldn't, or neglects to do something they should

> Wanting to release Jesus, Pilate appealed to them again. But they kept shouting, **"Crucify him! Crucify him!"**
> *(Luke 23: 20–21)*

> It was now about noon, and darkness came over the whole land until three in the afternoon, for the sun stopped shining. And the curtain of the temple was torn in two. Jesus called out with a loud voice, "Father, into your hands I commit my spirit." When he had said this, he breathed his last. The centurion, seeing what had happened, praised God and said, "Surely this was a righteous man."
> *(Luke 23: 44–47)*

For Christians, Jesus' death on the cross was proof of his humanity – he did actually die. This means that Jesus truly was God incarnate.

Christians believe Jesus' death was a sacrifice – his death brought about the forgiveness of humanity's **sins**. Through Jesus' death and resurrection, forgiveness becomes available to humanity and the loving relationship with God is restored (see 1.5).

Christians remember the crucifixion on Good Friday through worship, hymn-singing and prayers.

B An image from the 2004 film *The Passion of the Christ*, showing Jesus carrying the cross on which he is to be crucified

USEFUL TERMS

Ascension: going up into heaven

Resurrection: rising from the dead; also the view that after death God recreates a new body in a heavenly place

Jesus' resurrection

The Bible teaches that Jesus rose from the dead on the third day after he died. This is called the **resurrection**. For Christians, it shows that Jesus really was God and could overcome death.

A group of women went to Jesus' tomb to prepare his body for a proper burial. They discovered that the body had gone. According to the Bible, Jesus had risen:

> 'Why do you look for the living among the dead? **He is not here; he has risen!** Remember how he told you [...] The Son of Man must be delivered over to the hands of sinners, be crucified and on the third day be raised again.'
> *(Luke 24: 5–7)*

For Christians, this is important because it means that all Jesus taught is true. It means that humanity's sins are forgiven, people can have a true relationship with God again, and death is no longer the end. Christians believe that, if they believe in Jesus and follow his teachings, they will receive eternal life and be reunited with God. They remember the resurrection on Easter Sunday, which is a joyful celebration.

> '... you, with the help of wicked men, put him to death by nailing him to the cross. But **God raised him from the dead**, freeing him from the agony of death, because it was impossible for death to keep its hold on him.'
> *(Acts 2: 23–24)*

> '**Christ died for our sins** according to the scriptures, that he was buried, that he was raised on the third day...'
> *(1 Corinthians 15: 3–4)*

C According to the Bible, Jesus' tomb was found to be empty, with the large stone door rolled to one side

STRETCH

What does it mean to say that Jesus overcame death? Did Jesus die and then rise from the dead? Give reasons for your point of view. If Jesus didn't die, what do you think did happen?

Jesus' ascension

The Bible teaches that, after Jesus rose from the dead, he spent time teaching his disciples. He told them that he would soon be taken up to heaven (see 1.6) but that they would not be left alone. The Holy Spirit would come into the world and help them to spread the word of God.

> "... in a few days you will be baptised with the Holy Spirit. [...] You will receive power when the Holy Spirit comes on you; and you will be my witnesses in Jerusalem, and in all Judea and Samaria, and to the ends of the earth." After he said this, **he was taken up before their very eyes**, and a cloud hid him from their sight.
> *(Acts 1: 5–9)*

The last sentence of this quotation describes Jesus being taken up to heaven. This is called the **ascension**. Many Christians remember the ascension on Ascension Sunday through worship, hymn-singing and prayers.

D The ascension of Jesus depicted in a stained glass window in a Nottinghamshire church

BUILD YOUR SKILLS

1 Copy and complete the following table for the four important terms from the life and death of Jesus given in this unit.

Term	What does it mean?	Why is it important for Christians?
Last Supper		
Crucifixion		
Resurrection		
Ascension		

2 Consider whether you agree or disagree with each of the following statements and explain why.
- a 'Only Christians should be allowed to celebrate Christmas.'
- b 'Easter is about the death of Jesus, not about Easter eggs.'
- c 'Jesus did not exist.'
- d 'Jesus has no importance in today's world.'

3 Read Luke 22–24, taking notes about the key events. What can Christians learn about Jesus from these events? Write two paragraphs and explain your reasons using quotations.

SUMMARY

- Christians believe that Jesus is both God and man. They believe he was crucified, rose from the dead and, after a short time, ascended into heaven.
- Christians claim that all who believe in Jesus can have eternal life.
- Jesus taught people how to pray and how to have a relationship with God through love and worship.

EXAM-STYLE QUESTIONS

a Outline **three** events in the last days of Jesus' life. (3)

d 'Jesus' crucifixion was the most important event in history.' Evaluate this statement considering arguments for and against. In your response you should:
- refer to Christian teachings
- reach a justified conclusion. (15)

1.5 Salvation

SPECIFICATION FOCUS

The nature and significance of salvation and the role of Christ within salvation: law, sin, grace and Spirit, the role of Christ in salvation including John 3: 10–21 and Acts 4: 8–12; the nature and significance of atonement within Christianity and its link to salvation.

What is salvation?

Jesus Christ came to bring what Christians call **salvation**, by saving them from their sin and reuniting them with God. The Bible says:

> ‘For God did not send his Son into the world to condemn the world, but **to save the world** through him.’
> *(John 3: 17)*

So what does this mean? Christians believe that everyone was created for a relationship with God. Whether the account of Adam and Eve is taken as literal or not, it does show that humanity had a perfect relationship with God until they chose to walk away from it. Some Christians suggest that because Adam and Eve sinned against God, all humanity is automatically sinful and in need of salvation. Other Christians believe that people are not automatically sinful, but that all will sin at one time or another.

In many ways the nature of sin is not the primary focus of Christianity. The primary focus is on the God who loved humanity so much that he sent Jesus to die on the cross so that whoever believed in him would have a relationship with God forever (*John 3: 16*).

USEFUL TERMS

Atonement: the action of restoring a relationship; in Christianity, Jesus' death and resurrection restores the relationship between God and human beings

Grace: undeserved love

Law: guidelines as to how people should behave

Repentance: to say sorry for, and turn away from, any wrongdoing

Salvation: being saved from sin and the consequences of sin; going to **heaven** (see 1.6)

A A modern stained glass window in St Edmundsbury Cathedral showing an angel banishing Adam and Eve from the Garden of Eden

Law, sin, grace, and Spirit

Christians believe that people were separated from the love of God because they did wrongful things (sin) and disobeyed the **law** of God. The law consists of guidelines on how people should behave and the most famous part is the Ten Commandments (*Exodus 20*).

However, Jesus taught that the law was not enough to save people (*Matthew 5: 20*) and he was critical of those who congratulated themselves on keeping the law (*Luke 5: 32*). What was needed was **repentance** and an acceptance that righteousness was not possible without the **grace** that came through Jesus.

In other words, people might think that by trying really hard to be good they can achieve God's favour, but this is not the case in the Christian faith. In the Book of Acts, the Apostle Peter explains that the only way that people can be saved is through Jesus:

> '**Salvation is found in no one else**, for there is no other name under heaven given to mankind by which we must be saved.'
> *(Acts 4: 12)*

Christians therefore believe that they must turn away from sin, receive the freely given gift of grace through Jesus, and have faith in him, in order to be saved. Christians believe that, when they make this decision for the first time, they also welcome the Holy Spirit into their lives.

B *Christ of Saint John of the Cross* by Salvador Dalí (1951)

What is atonement?

Christians believe that, because Jesus died to save humanity from sin, the relationship between God and humanity was restored. This is called **atonement** or, more literally, 'at-one-ment'. God and humans are 'at one' because of Jesus.

Christians believe Jesus died as an act of love to save humanity, even though humanity did not deserve it. His love is called grace, which means undeserved love.

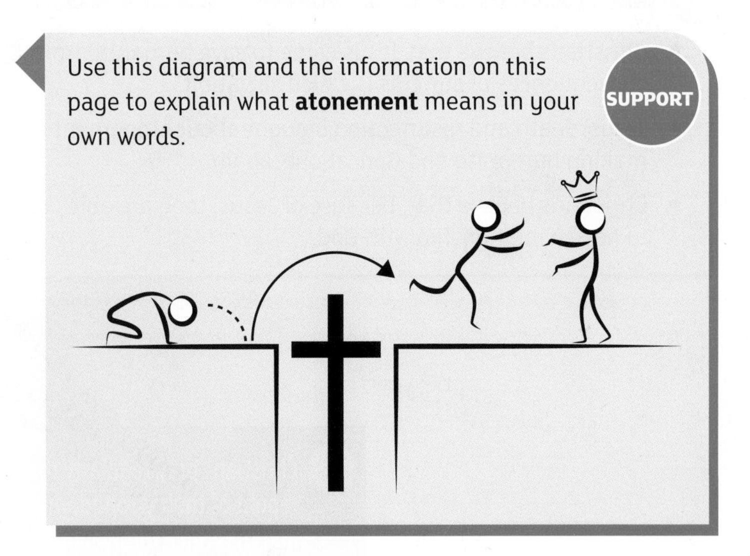

What is the significance of atonement and salvation within Christianity?

- Christians believe Jesus' death allows humans to have eternal life.
- Christians have a moral duty to live their lives as Jesus lived his, loving and caring for each other: 'I have set you an example that you should do as I have done for you.' (*John 13: 15*). In this way, humans are saved from the power and consequences of sin.
- God and humanity can have their loving relationship restored. Christians regularly repent of any wrongdoing and believe that, because of Jesus, they are forgiven by God.

BUILD YOUR SKILLS

1 Complete the following table concerning salvation:

Term	What does it mean?	Why is it important for Christians?
Sin		
Salvation		
Sacrifice		
Atonement		

2 Read through this topic carefully and write an answer to each of the following questions, making sure you explain your points:

a Why did the Son of God come to earth as a human?
b Why doesn't God just forgive sins?
c Do you believe humans need the salvation that Jesus offers?
d How does atonement link to salvation?

EXAM-STYLE QUESTIONS

a Outline **three** features of salvation for Christians. (3)
c Explain **two** reasons why salvation is important for Christians today. In your answer you must refer to a source of wisdom and authority. (5)

SUMMARY

- Christians believe that Jesus came to save humanity from the consequences of sin; this is called salvation.
- Jesus' death and resurrection brought about atonement – making humanity and God 'at one' again.
- Christians believe that, because of Jesus, they are able to have a relationship with God.

C Christians pray regularly to repent of their wrongdoings and to receive forgiveness from God

1.6 Christian eschatology

Eschatology is an area of Christian teaching which is all about life after death. All living things eventually die, but Christians believe that there is another life beyond this physical life. Here are a few Christian beliefs.

When we die, the souls of the good go to a wonderful paradise called **heaven** to be with God.

When we die, the souls of the wicked go to a place of eternal punishment called **hell**.

On the Last Day, God will raise the dead in bodily form. This is resurrection.

The Bible teaches that all who believe in Jesus will have eternal life:

> 'For God so loved the world that he gave his one and only Son, that **whoever believes in him shall not perish but have eternal life.**'
> *(John 3: 16)*

Christians think of life after death in divergent ways:

- The most common view is that everyone has an **immortal soul** that leaves our physical body when we die and goes to God in heaven, or otherwise goes to hell. This view holds that followers of Jesus who die will go to heaven and those who are not followers of Jesus will go to hell. Christians differ on what they think heaven and hell will be like.
- Some Christians believe that Jesus died to forgive all sins, and so everyone (not just Christians) will live forever in heaven. This is called **universalism**.
- Many Catholics believe in **purgatory**, where the dead are purified of their sins before going to heaven.

Christians also vary on whether the above happens as soon as people die, or at the end of time, on what Christians call the **Day of Judgement**.

Heaven

Heaven is the place where Christians believe that they will spend the afterlife. It is not described in detail in the Bible, so Christians have different views about what it will be like. Some believe that it is a physical place, whilst others believe it is a state of being spiritually united with God. The Bible teaches that heaven is a place of everlasting peace and joy for those who believe in Jesus:

> 'Then I saw "a new heaven and a new earth" [...] I saw the Holy City, the new Jerusalem, coming down out of heaven from God [...] He will wipe every tear from their eyes. There will be no more death or mourning or crying or pain...'
> *(Revelation 21: 1–4)*

SPECIFICATION FOCUS

Christian eschatology: divergent Christian teachings about life after death, including the nature and significance of resurrection, judgement, heaven, and hell and purgatory with reference to the 39 Articles of Religion and Catholic teachings; how beliefs about life after death are shown in the Bible, including reference to 2 Corinthians 5: 1–10 and divergent understandings as to why they are important for Christians today.

USEFUL TERMS

Day of Judgement: time when God assesses a person's life and actions

Eschatology: an area of Christian theology which is concerned with life after death

Heaven: place of eternal paradise where Christians believe they will spend the afterlife

Hell: place of punishment and separation from God

Immortal soul: a soul that lives on after the death of the physical body

Purgatory: a place where the souls of the dead are cleansed and prepared for heaven

Universalism: the belief that because of the love and mercy of God everyone will go to heaven

A

Hell

Many Christians believe in hell, a place of punishment and separation from God. Some Christians do not believe in hell, and instead believe that those who are not followers of Jesus would simply cease to exist when they die. Like heaven, the descriptions of hell in the Bible are not detailed:

> 'He will punish those who do not know God and do not obey the gospel of our Lord Jesus. They will be punished with everlasting destruction...'
> *(2 Thessalonians 1: 8–9)*

Purgatory

Purgatory, from the Latin word *purgare* meaning 'make clean', is a concept mainly associated with the Catholic Church. It is a place (or state of mind) where the souls of those who have died go to be purified until they are made clean from their sins and can then go to heaven. The *Catechism of the Catholic Church* describes it in this way:

> 'All who die in God's grace and friendship, but still imperfectly purified, are indeed assured of their eternal salvation; but **after death they undergo purification**, so as to achieve the holiness necessary to enter the joy of heaven.'
> *Catechism of the Catholic Church, 1030*

However, this is not a view held by Protestant Christians. The *39 Articles of Religion*, which is an ancient statement of the beliefs and teachings of the Church of England, says the following about purgatory:

> 'The Romish Doctrine concerning Purgatory [...] is a fond thing vainly invented, and grounded upon no warranty of Scripture, but rather repugnant to the Word of God.'
> *(Article 22, 39 Articles of Religion)*

SUPPORT

This is a strongly worded criticism of the idea of purgatory:

- '**Fond thing vainly invented**' means they believe it has been made up
- '**Grounded upon no warranty of Scripture**' means they don't believe it is backed up by the Bible
- '**Repugnant**' means unacceptable.

Judgement

Christians believe that God is just, fair and merciful. They believe in the Day of Judgement, when God will judge all people according to how they lived their lives on earth and to give them the afterlife they deserve.

> 'And I saw the dead, great and small, standing before the throne [...] the dead were judged according to what they had done...'
> *(Revelation 20: 12)*

Christians also believe in the Second Coming, when Jesus will return to earth. This will be the time for judgement and the establishment of God's kingdom.

C At Christian funerals, mourners are reminded of the promise of eternal life

Resurrection

For Christians, the resurrection of Jesus has made sure that there will be an afterlife for all who believe in him. In *1 Corinthians 15: 12*, St Paul wrote, 'But if it is preached that Christ has been raised from the dead, how can some of you say that there is no resurrection of the dead?' Paul argues that if Christians believe that Jesus rose from the dead, then they must believe they can look forward to an afterlife.

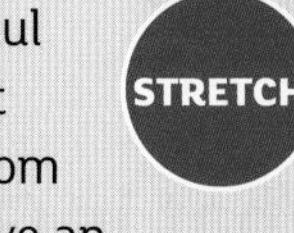

What do you think Paul means by saying that because Jesus rose from the dead they can have an afterlife?

Therefore, many Christians believe that, at the end of time, God will raise their bodies to life again, as he did with Jesus' body. The appearances of Jesus after his resurrection are usually thought by Christians to be the strongest evidence that this will happen. According to the Bible, when Jesus appeared to his disciples after death they were able to touch him *(Luke 24: 39)*. Paul uses the metaphor of buildings to explain what will happen to the body after death:

> 'For we know that if the earthly tent we live in is destroyed, we have a building from God, an eternal house in heaven, not built by human hands.'
> *(2 Corinthians 5: 1)*

In other words, the physical human body eventually dies, but a resurrected body goes on forever.

Why is life after death important for Christians today?

- Jesus said that those who believe in him would have life after death.
- Life after death is a reward for faithful people.
- Life after death offers hope for the future.
- Life after death allows Christians to be with God forever.

COMPARE AND CONTRAST

In your exam, you could be asked to **compare and contrast** Christian beliefs on life after death with the beliefs of another religion you are studying. You should consider the similarities and differences between them.

BUILD YOUR SKILLS

1 Look at images **A** and **B**. How successful are they at depicting heaven and hell? Explain your reasons and refer to Christian beliefs.

2 Here are some divergent views about life after death.
- 'If God really loves us, everyone should go to heaven.'
- 'There is no life after death. When we die, we just die.'
- 'People who are bad should go to hell as a punishment.'

a Consider whether you agree or disagree with each statement and explain why.

b How might a religious believer respond to each statement?

SUMMARY

- Christian belief in the afterlife is very important and is connected to beliefs about Jesus' own death and resurrection and what that means for Christians.
- There are divergent views within Christianity about the nature of heaven and hell, purgatory, and the resurrection of the body.

EXAM-STYLE QUESTIONS

b Describe **two** differences between Christian beliefs on life after death and those of another religion you have studied. (4)

d 'There is no life after death.' Evaluate this statement considering arguments for and against. In your response you should:
- refer to Christian teachings
- refer to different Christian points of view
- reach a justified conclusion.

(15)

1.7 The problem of evil

SPECIFICATION FOCUS

The problem of evil/suffering and a loving and righteous God: the problems it raises for Christians about the nature of God, including reference to omnipotence and benevolence, including Psalm 103; how the problem may cause believers to question their faith or the existence of God; the nature and examples of natural suffering, moral suffering.

What is God like?

There are two characteristics of God's nature that are particularly important in helping Christians to approach the problem of evil and suffering:

- **Omnipotence** – God is all-powerful
- **Benevolence** – God is all-good/loving.

Christians believe that, if God is all-powerful, then nothing is impossible for him; if he is all-good, then he is loving and cannot do wrong. In the Bible, God's love and power means that he not only *wants* to help people, but he is also *able* to:

> 'The Lord works righteousness and justice for all the oppressed'
> *(Psalm 103: 6)*

What is the problem of evil and suffering?

Evil is the opposite of good: it causes pain, grief and damage. Evil and suffering can be on a large scale or a smaller, personal scale, as almost everyone experiences pain and suffering at different times in their lives.

There are two types of evil and suffering:

- **Natural evil**: suffering caused by nature that is beyond human control.
- **Moral evil**: deliberately evil actions by human beings that cause suffering to others.

USEFUL TERMS

Benevolence: all-good

Moral evil: suffering caused by humans, such as war

Natural evil: suffering caused by natural events, such as earthquakes

Omnipotence: all-powerful

A Examples of natural evil; image shows a man rescuing an unknown girl from flood waters in Bangkok

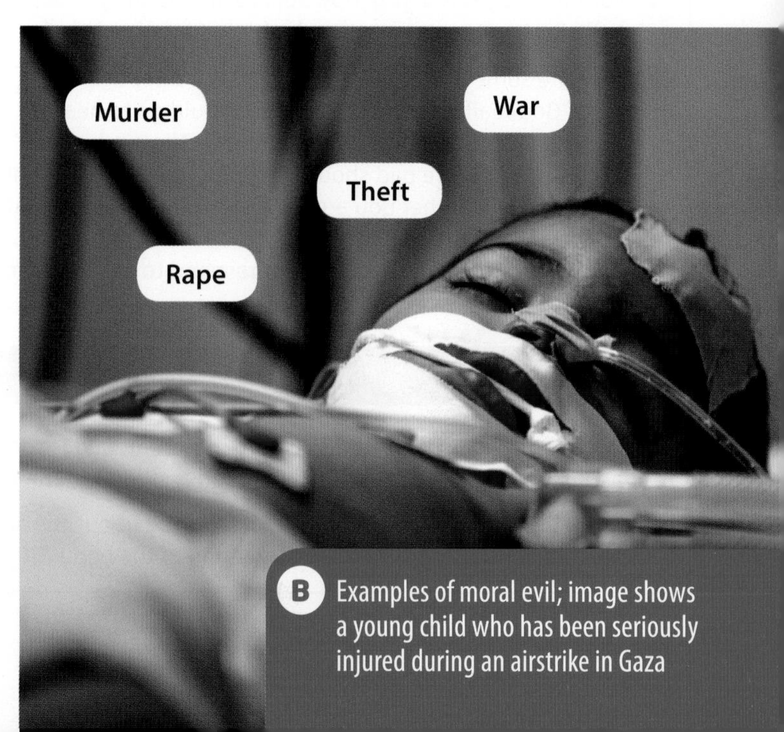

B Examples of moral evil; image shows a young child who has been seriously injured during an airstrike in Gaza

How might the problem lead some people to question God's existence?

The existence of evil and suffering in the world is one of the strongest arguments against the existence of God. If it is true that God is all-powerful and all-loving, it seems logical that he should prevent evil and suffering. Since evil and suffering *do* exist, some people have concluded that God does *not*.

The problem can be expressed in this way:

- God is thought to be all-loving (benevolent) and all-powerful (omnipotent).
- If God is benevolent he would *want* to remove evil and suffering.
- If God is omnipotent he would *be able* to remove evil and suffering.
- Therefore, both God and evil cannot exist together, yet evil *does* exist.
- Therefore, God cannot exist.

This can be illustrated in the form of an inconsistent triad (see image **C**).

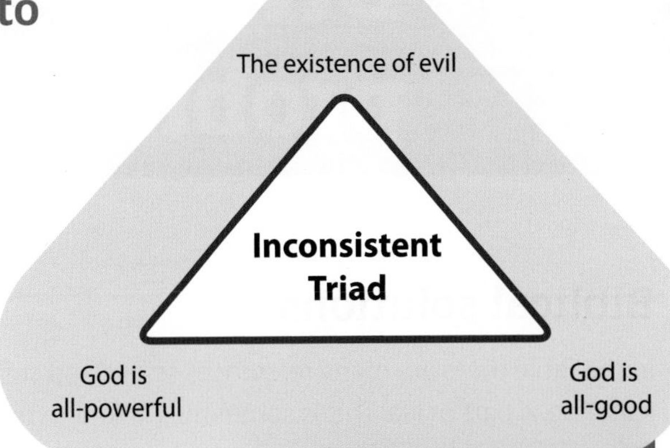

C The inconsistent triad; if you combine any two points of the triangle, the third point is disproved

Why does the problem cause believers to question their faith?

The problem of evil challenges the existence and characteristics of God. This can cause believers to doubt their beliefs, especially if they or their loved ones are experiencing pain. In times of doubt, a Christian might ask:

- If God exists but isn't all-powerful and all-loving, how can I worship him?
- If God is not all-powerful or not all-loving, is that a God I want to believe in?
- If God is all-powerful and all-loving, how could he allow suffering?

SUPPORT

Many people find it difficult to understand what it means to say that God is all-loving. Some believe God should only love those who are good. If God is all-loving, does he love tyrants and mass murderers?

BUILD YOUR SKILLS

1. What are the two kinds of evil? Can you give five examples of each kind?  **SUPPORT**
2. Write down a potential problem of God's omnipotence.
   a. How would a non-religious person respond?
   b. How would a Christian respond?
3. a. Is a God who is not all-powerful still worthy of a Christian's worship? Why/why not?  **STRETCH**
   b. If God is benevolent, can he ever be bad?

SUMMARY

- Christians believe that God is omnipotent and benevolent.
- There are two types of evil in the world: natural evil and moral evil.
- Some people question whether the existence of evil and suffering shows that God either does not exist or is not all-powerful or all-loving.

EXAM-STYLE QUESTIONS

a. Outline **three** features of the problem of evil and suffering. (3)
b. Explain **two** types of evil and suffering. (4)

1.8 Divergent solutions to the problem of evil

SPECIFICATION FOCUS

Divergent solutions offered to the problem of evil/suffering and a loving and righteous God: biblical, theoretical and practical, including reference to Psalm 119, Job, free will, vale of soul-making, prayer, and charity; the success of solutions to the problem.

Biblical solutions

In the Bible there are many references to evil and suffering, and suggestions that suffering is part of life. This is sometimes linked to the existence of a personal force of evil, given different names in the history of Christianity: the Devil, **Satan** or Lucifer. In Christianity, Satan (which means 'the adversary') was one of God's angels who had rebelled against the rule of God. In the Book of Job, a good man and a believer in God suffers great hardship and tragedy after God is challenged by Satan.

> 'What I feared has come upon me;
> **what I dreaded has happened to me.**
> I have no peace, no quietness.
> I have no rest, but only turmoil.'
> *(Job 3: 25–26)*

USEFUL TERMS

Satan: 'the adversary'; one of God's angels who rebelled against the rule of God

In the midst of Job's suffering, God tells him that the problem of evil and suffering has no simple answer and that he must trust God. In the end, all turns out well for Job.

> 'The fear of the Lord – that is wisdom,
> and to shun evil is understanding.'
> *(Job 28: 28)*

> 'I know that you [God] can do all things;
> no purpose of yours can be thwarted.'
> *(Job 42: 2)*

STRETCH

The story of Job is very complex and raises questions. If God is all-powerful, why does he allow Satan to tell him what to do or exist at all? If God is all-loving, why does he permit the suffering of a good man? The answer seems to be that God is mysterious and humans are not allowed to know everything. What do you think?

A This child has no parents and no home, and has to beg on the streets of Mumbai in order to survive. For some people, the question of why suffering happens has no easy answer.

The Book of Psalms is a collection of songs and prayers dedicated to God in which the theme of suffering is very common. Some of the psalms express feelings of abandonment by God:

> ‘Save me, O God, for the waters have come up to my neck. [...] I am worn out calling for help; my throat is parched. **My eyes fail, looking for my God.**’
> *(Psalm 69: 1, 3)*

Psalm 119 acknowledges the existence of suffering as part of life, but also states that God is trustworthy:

> ‘My comfort in my suffering is this: Your promise preserves my life.’
> *(Psalm 119: 50)*
>
> ‘My soul faints with longing for your salvation, but I have put my hope in your word.’
> *(Psalm 119: 81)*

Other psalms praise God for his help in times of trouble:

> ‘**I called to the Lord**, who is worthy of praise,
> **and I have been saved** from my enemies.’
> *(Psalm 18: 3)*

The Bible teaches that, one day, God will end all evil and suffering for good:

> ‘**He will wipe every tear from their eyes**. There will be no more death or mourning or crying or pain, for the old order of things has passed away.’
> *(Revelation 21: 4)*

Biblical solutions to evil and suffering encourage Christians to believe:

- Suffering is part of life.
- Christians can pray to God to get comfort in their suffering and they should praise God for his help in times of trouble.
- God is love, but sometimes it's hard to understand why God doesn't intervene. Faith sometimes involves trust without understanding.
- One day all suffering will come to an end.

B A mother and child light a candle in an Orthodox church; many Christians light candles when they pray as a symbol of Jesus bringing hope in times of darkness

Theoretical solutions

Christians may respond by looking at what is behind the problem and how it may be resolved. In the Bible, *Genesis 2–3* highlights this very clearly by showing that evil and suffering can be the result of human free will. The first human beings, Adam and Eve, used their free will to disobey God. When they did so, evil and suffering were brought into the world and they were separated from God.

> ‘So the Lord God banished him [Adam] from the garden of Eden to work the ground from which he had been taken.’
> *(Genesis 3: 23)*

Some Christians go further and say that this world is a **vale of soul-making** – an environment where everything that is necessary for human growth and development can be found. For instance, in the midst of evil and suffering there are opportunities to do good, or to do bad, to choose the right way or the wrong way.

Theoretical solutions to evil and suffering encourage Christians to believe:

- God gives humans free will to act as they wish.
- Humans may choose to do evil or inflict suffering and that's why evil exists.
- Suffering helps people to develop good characteristics.

USEFUL TERMS

Intercession: prayers for those who are suffering

Vale of soul-making: an environment in which human beings can overcome evil by making good choices

SUPPORT

Some Christians say that the world provides all they need to choose to be good or bad people. Can you think of some examples?

Practical responses

Christians believe that suffering is part of life, and they have a duty to respond to this practically:

- They can develop positive qualities such as compassion and kindness, courage and honesty.
- They can help each other to make the world a better place and learn how to improve things for themselves and future generations.
- They can help through involvement in charity work.
- They can pray for God's help and encouragement.

Many Christians pray for those who are suffering. This is called **intercession**. They believe that they can change the impacts of evil and suffering by praying to God on behalf of those who are suffering.

Practical responses to evil and suffering encourage Christians to believe:

- Christians can develop positive qualities such as compassion.
- Suffering is part of life but help can be given.
- Christians can help by praying and doing charitable work.

C Many Christians meet together to pray in times of difficulty

The success of solutions to the problem

	Strengths	Weaknesses
Biblical solutions	• Help Christians to understand God more clearly and trust that he will make everything right in the end. • Help Christians to believe that God acts for good in the world.	• People in the Bible still experience suffering, and God does not always stop it. • It can be harder to trust God when things aren't going well.
Theoretical solutions	• Explain that evil and suffering come from human free will, not from God. • Encourage Christians to use times of evil and suffering to make the right choices and grow closer to God.	• God created the universe, therefore he must be responsible for the existence of evil. • It may not be reasonable to expect people to respond well in times of suffering.
Practical responses	Christians would say that practical responses to evil and suffering are not a 'solution' to the problem, but they can be successful in easing suffering. Christians believe suffering is a reality of life, and they have a choice to respond practically to help with the consequences.	

BUILD YOUR SKILLS

1. Of the solutions to the problem of evil and suffering,
   a. which is the most successful?
   b. which is the least successful?

   Give your reasons.
2. Would the world be a better place if there was no evil and suffering? Discuss with a partner.
3. Look through a newspaper and make a list of all the news stories involving suffering. Then answer these questions:

   STRETCH

   a. What was the suffering shown in each incident?
   b. Was the suffering in each case an act of nature or caused by human actions?
   c. How could the suffering in each case have been prevented?
   d. Do you think that prayer would be useful in these situations? Think carefully about what you think prayer accomplishes.

SUMMARY

- The problem of evil and suffering challenges the existence of God because if God is all-good and all-powerful, why doesn't he put an end to suffering?
- Christians respond to evil and suffering in different ways, including reading the Bible, praying, and working to relieve suffering.
- Christians might argue that God gave humans free will, and that evil and suffering are the consequences of human action.

EXAM-STYLE QUESTIONS

c. Explain **two** different Christian solutions to the problem of evil and suffering. In your answer you must refer to a source of wisdom and authority. (5)

d. 'God is not responsible for suffering in the world.' Evaluate this statement considering arguments for and against. In your response you should:
   - refer to Christian teachings
   - refer to different Christian points of view
   - reach a justified conclusion. (15)

Revision

BUILD YOUR SKILLS

Look at the list of 'I can' statements below and think carefully about how confident you are. Use the following code to rate each of the statements. Be honest!

Green – very confident. What is your evidence for this?

Orange – quite confident. What is your target? Be specific.

Red – not confident. What is your target? Be specific.

A self-assessment revision checklist is available on *Kerboodle*

I can...

- Explain what the Trinity is and why the oneness of God is significant
- Give reasons why the Trinity is significant in Christianity
- Give quotations from the Bible and the Nicene Creed about the Trinity
- Explain the characteristics of the Trinity – Father, Son, and Holy Spirit
- Describe how the Trinity is reflected in Christian worship and belief today
- Describe the biblical account of creation
- Explain two different ways that Christians interpret creation
- Explain the role of the Word and Spirit in creation with reference to sources of wisdom and authority
- Explain the importance of creation for Christians today
- Explain the meaning of the incarnation with reference to a source of wisdom and authority
- Explain why the incarnation is so important to Christians
- Describe the key events in the last days of Jesus' life (including the Last Supper, betrayal, arrest, trial, crucifixion, resurrection and ascension of Jesus), with reference to the accounts of these within the Bible
- Give reasons why these events are significant, and describe what they show about the person of Jesus
- Explain the idea of salvation and why it is so important within Christianity
- Explain the role of Jesus in salvation including reference to a source of wisdom and authority
- Define atonement, and explain how it links to salvation
- Explain different Christian views on life after death
- Explain the meaning and significance of resurrection, judgement, heaven, hell, and purgatory with reference to sources of wisdom and authority
- Describe the problem of evil and suffering, with reference to natural and moral evil
- Explain the problems suffering raises for Christians about the nature of God
- Explain how evil and suffering can challenge religious belief
- Describe different solutions to the problem of evil and suffering, including biblical, theoretical and practical solutions
- Discuss the success of the solutions to the problem of evil.

Exam practice

On these exam practice pages you will see example answers for each of the exam question types: **a**, **b**, **c**, and **d**. You can find out more about these on pages 6–11.

• Question 'a'

*Question **a** is AO1 – this tests your knowledge and understanding.*

(a) Outline **three** features of the biblical story of creation. (3)

Student response

God created the earth in six days and then he rested.

WHAT WENT WELL

This student has correctly identified an aspect of the biblical story of creation.

HOW TO IMPROVE

This answer does not outline three features of the biblical story of creation. For a high level response, three distinct features should be given. See the 'improved student response' opposite for suggested corrections.

Improved student response

The biblical story of creation says that God is the creator. He created the earth in six days and then rested. He looked at his creation and decided that it was good.

Over to you! Give yourself three minutes on the clock and have a go at answering this question. Remember, this question type requires you to provide three facts or short ideas: you don't need to explain them or express any opinions.

• Question 'b'

*Question **b** is AO1 – this tests your knowledge and understanding.*

(a) Explain **two** Christian beliefs about the incarnation. (4)

Student response

The Son of God came to earth, and he was born a human called Jesus.

WHAT WENT WELL

The student has given a correct Christian belief and explained it.

HOW TO IMPROVE

The question asks for two Christian beliefs about the incarnation, and the answer only contains one. For a high level response, students should explain two Christian beliefs about the incarnation. See the 'improved student response' opposite for suggested corrections.

Improved student response

The incarnation is a core Christian doctrine which holds that the Son of God came to earth, and he was born a human called Jesus.

Christians also believe that the incarnation took place for a special purpose, which was to restore the relationship between God and humanity which had been destroyed by sin.

Over to you! Give yourself four minutes on the clock and have a go at answering this question. Remember, in order to 'explain' something, you need to **develop** your points. See page 9 for a reminder of how to do this.

• Question 'c'

*Question **c** is A01 – this tests your knowledge and understanding.*

(c) Explain **two** different Christian beliefs about life after death. In your answer you must refer to a source of wisdom and authority. (5)

Student response

Roman Catholic Christians believe in the existence of purgatory, a place where the souls of the dead go to be purified after death. This is so that they can achieve holiness before entering heaven.

The Church of England does not believe in the existence of purgatory however, and argues that it is not referred to in the Bible.

WHAT WENT WELL

This student has correctly explained two different Christian beliefs about life after death.

HOW TO IMPROVE

The student hasn't referred to a source of wisdom and authority. See the 'improved student response' opposite for a suggested correction.

Improved student response

Roman Catholic Christians believe in the existence of purgatory, a place where the souls of the dead go to be purified after death. This is so that they can achieve holiness before entering heaven.

The Church of England does not believe in the existence of purgatory however, and argues that it is not referred to in the Bible. The 39 Articles of Religion claim that it has been 'invented' (Article 22).

Over to you! Give yourself five minutes on the clock and have a go at answering this question. Remember, you need to write two developed points, one of which needs to be supported by a source of wisdom and authority.

• Question 'd'

*Question **d** is A02 – this tests your ability to evaluate. Some 'd' questions also carry an extra three marks for spelling, punctuation and grammar.*

In this question, 3 of the marks awarded will be for your spelling, punctuation and grammar and your use of specialist terminology.

*(d) 'Christianity provides no solutions to the problem of evil and suffering.' Evaluate this statement considering arguments for and against. In your response you should:

- refer to Christian teachings
- refer to different Christian points of view
- reach a justified conclusion. (15)

Student response

If God was benevolent he would not let us suffer. Christains will teach that God knows why people suffer, consequently he uses suffering to show his love and faithfulness to people and this should give them faith.

The Catholic Church teaches that it is a Christian responsibility to respond in practical ways to ease the suffering of others. Because of this many Christians will choose jobs which show they care and help other people.

However some Christians could argue that evil and suffering has nothing to do with God as in the Bible it says evil is a result of the actions of Adam and Eve. Therefore it is not a Christian's duty to provide solutions for the problem of evil and suffering.

WHAT WENT WELL

This is a low level response. The student understands that they must explain different Christian viewpoints.

HOW TO IMPROVE

Both sides of this argument lack detailed understanding, and there aren't any clear links back to the question. It could be improved with a more logical chain of reasoning, and more detail, including specific references to sources of wisdom and authority. There is also a spelling error. See the 'improved student response' opposite for suggested corrections.

Improved student response

For many Christians, the way they respond to suffering is a very important part of their faith. They believe that suffering brings them closer to God as Christians will teach that God knows why people suffer, consequently he uses suffering to show his love and faithfulness to his followers. It could be argued, however, that the existence of evil and suffering in the world challenges the claim that Christianity has anything to offer, because the problem is yet to be solved.

In contrast to this view, the existence of evil and suffering is seen by many as proof that Christians have a duty to help each other and relieve suffering in whichever way is needed. The Catholic Church teaches that it is a Christian responsibility to respond in practical ways to ease the suffering of others through charitable actions. Because of this many Christians will choose jobs which show they care and want to help other people.

However, some Christians think that the problem of evil and suffering is a direct result of the misuse of human free will and therefore has nothing to do with God. The story of the Fall places responsibility for suffering on humanity: "Cursed is the ground because of you" (Genesis 3: 17), which suggests that it is the responsibility of humans to find solutions to reducing suffering in the world.

On balance, it seems to me that the Christian faith does have solutions to offer. Salvation can only be achieved if Christians consider their actions and how they support others and this is most evident when faced with suffering.

Over to you! Give yourself 15 minutes on the clock and have a go at answering this question. Remember to refer back to the original statement in your writing when you give different points of view, and make sure you cover each of the bullet points given in the question. Allow three minutes to check your spelling, punctuation and grammar and use of specialist terminology.

BUILD YOUR SKILLS

In your exams, you'll need to make sure you use religious terminology correctly. Do you know the meaning of the following important terms for this topic?

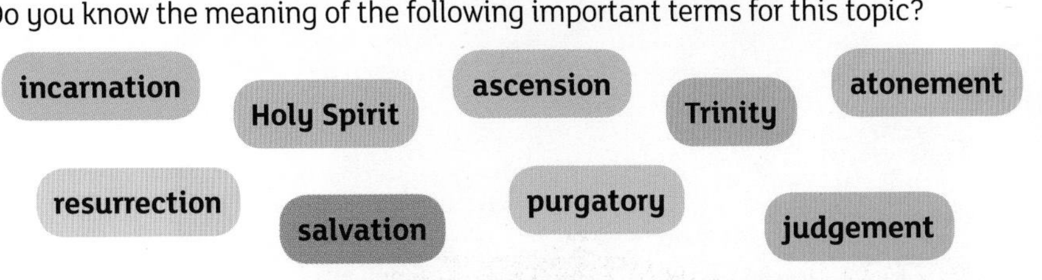

Chapter 2: Marriage and the Family

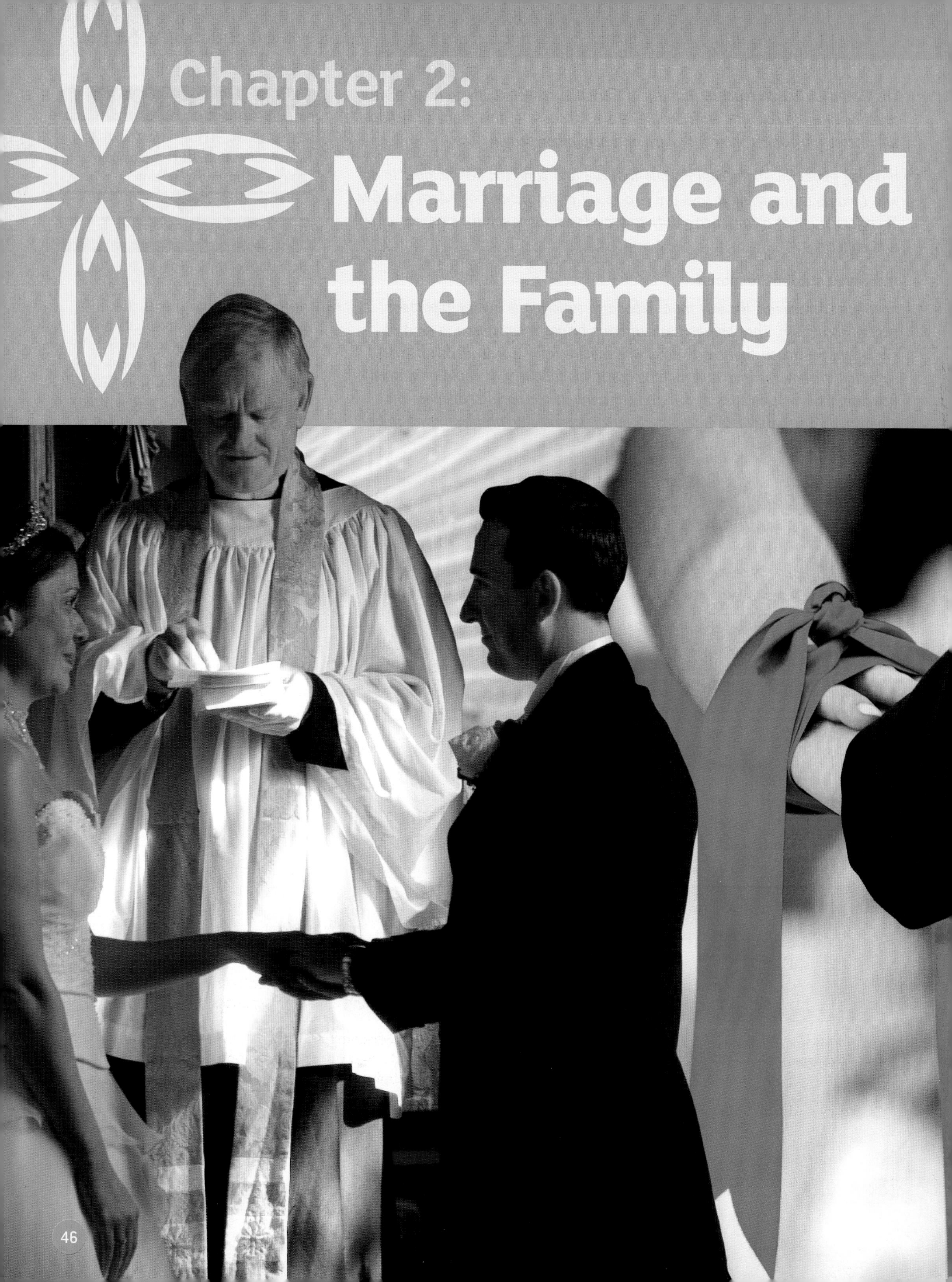

2.1 Marriage

SPECIFICATION FOCUS

The importance and purpose of marriage for Christians: Christian teachings about the significance of marriage in Christian life; the purpose of marriage for Christians including Mark 10: 6–9; divergent Christian and non-religious (including atheist and Humanist) attitudes to the importance of marriage in society; including the sanctity of marriage, a lack of importance, cohabitation and Christian responses to these attitudes.

Marriage in society

Marriage is the public commitment between two people. On the whole it is the public commitment between two people who love each other, but this is not the case in all cultures. Marriage is a legal state, but it is also given great significance within virtually all world religions.

Marriage is a lifelong union of two people that can only be ended by the death of one partner, by **divorce**, or by **annulment**. For a couple who are attracted to each other, who talk together and share interests, respect, value and support each other, marriage is often seen as the culmination of that loving relationship.

In the United Kingdom, there are three legal requirements that must be fulfilled before a marriage can take place.

- Both partners must be over 16 years old (and, if under 18 years, have their parents' consent).
- Neither partner must be already married to someone else (being married to multiple partners is called bigamy and is illegal in most countries).
- Both partners must enter into the marriage freely, not under threat.

Since July 2013 same-sex marriages have been legal in the UK and the first same-sex wedding ceremonies took place in March 2014.

Why is marriage important in society?

Society values marriage for several reasons:

- it structures society into family groups which can form the basis of culture and community
- it encourages stability
- it provides a secure environment for bringing up children
- it provides legal protection for both partners and their children
- it nurtures feelings of self-esteem and value
- it has value both for religious and non-religious people.

A A same-sex couple on their wedding day

What do Christians believe about marriage?

Christians believe in the **sanctity of marriage** – that marriage is a holy gift from God in which partners make a commitment to each other to live together in an exclusive loving relationship until the death of one of them. This is called **faithfulness** – promising to have sexual relations only with the marriage partner. For many Christians, for example Catholics, marriage is also a sacrament (see 3.2), which is a very important Christian ceremony officially recognised by the Church as having been established by Jesus.

Jesus' teaching on marriage is set out in Mark's Gospel:

> 'But at the beginning of creation God "made them male and female". "For this reason a man will **leave his father and mother** and be united to his wife, and **the two will become one flesh**." So they are no longer two, but one flesh. Therefore **what God has joined together let no one separate**.'
> *(Mark 10: 6–9)*

This is based on an Old Testament text:

> 'That is why a man leaves his father and mother and is united to his wife, and they become one flesh.'
> *(Genesis 2: 24)*

Most Christians draw four main points from Jesus' teaching.

- God intended from creation that men and women should marry.
- Marriage becomes the most important adult relationship that the partners have.
- Marriage creates a unity ('one flesh') which is physical and emotional.
- The couple are joined together by God and their relationship should be respected by others.

USEFUL TERMS

Annulment: declaration that a marriage is null and void; in effect, as if it had never happened, for reasons such as being under age or being forced to marry

Divorce: the legal ending of a marriage

Faithfulness: not having a sexual relationship with anyone other than a partner

Marriage: the legal union of a man and a woman or a same-sex couple

Sanctity of marriage: the idea that marriage has special significance as a holy gift from God

STRETCH

The Bible teaches that there is an order within the marriage relationship, in which the husband is the head of the wife (see 2.7). He must love and honour her and she, in turn, is to respect and honour him: 'Wives, submit yourselves to your husbands as you do to the Lord. For the husband is the head of the wife as Christ is the head of the church [...] Husbands, love your wives, just as Christ loved the church' *(Ephesians 5: 22–25)*.

Because the Bible teaches that marriage is a union between a man and a woman, the Church has to deal with many different views on whether same-sex marriages should be accepted by the Church. There is more about this later in the chapter.

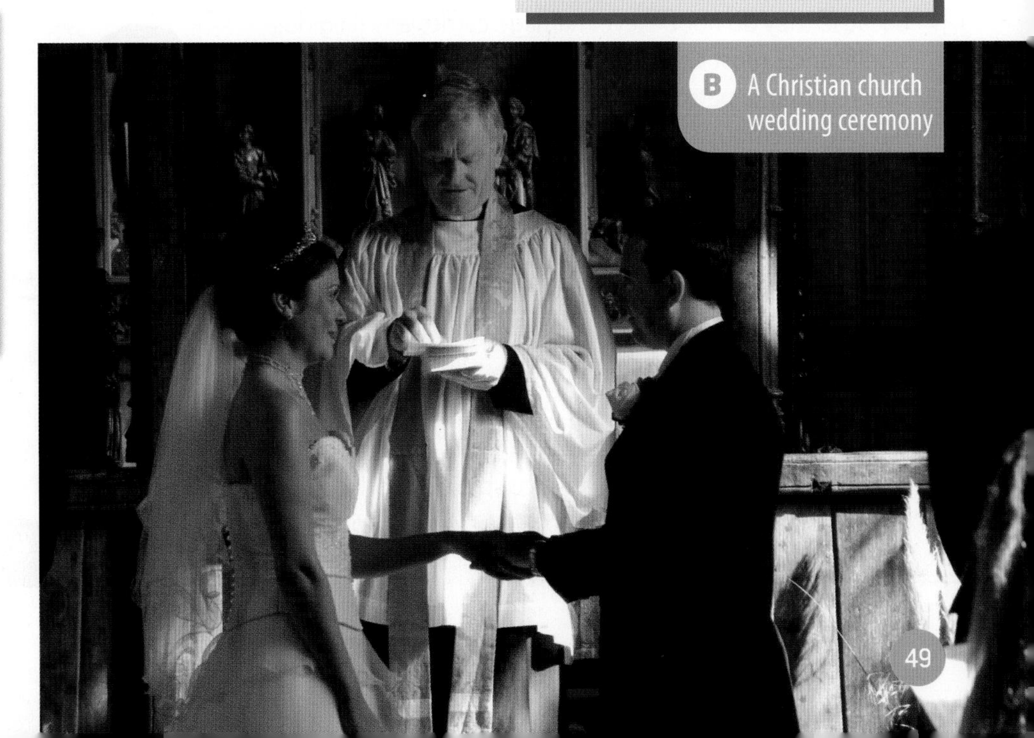

B A Christian church wedding ceremony

What is cohabitation?

In the UK today, about half of all couples choose to live together without being married – this is called **cohabitation**. In 2016 the UK National Statistics Office revealed that the cohabiting family is the fastest growing family type. Some cohabiting couples decide after a while of having lived together to get married, whereas others may cohabit without ever marrying.

Those who are in favour of cohabitation might argue the following:

- it enables couples to get to know each other properly before making the commitment of marriage
- if the relationship doesn't work, they can separate without the legal consequences of divorce
- children can be brought up as successfully by a cohabiting couple as by a married couple
- marriage lacks importance: a couple can make a loving personal commitment to each other without going through a legal ceremony.

However, others who are against cohabitation, for example many Christians, might argue the following:

- it can encourage a casual attitude towards relationships
- it is too easy to break up and so couples are not encouraged to talk things through when times get tough
- children are best brought up in a stable home with two married parents
- the Bible supports lifelong marriage.

USEFUL TERMS

Atheist: someone who does not believe in the existence of God

Cohabitation: living together in a sexual relationship but without legalising the union through marriage

Humanist: a non-religious person who looks to reason and empathy in order to live a meaningful life

What do non-religious people believe about marriage?

- Many non-religious people also believe that marriage can be a way of two people showing publicly their loving commitment to one another. However, they do not believe that it carries any religious significance.
- Because they do not believe marriage carries any religious significance, most **atheists** choose a civil ceremony conducted by a registrar (a person authorised by law to carry out legally binding ceremonies) in any place licensed for weddings.
- There is a specific **Humanist** wedding service, but at present Humanist marriage ceremonies are recognised only in law in Scotland, and not in the rest of the UK. However, Humanist couples may choose to have a legal marriage by a registrar as well as a Humanist celebration.
- Like Christians, many atheists and Humanists value faithfulness within their marriage, but there is no rule about this. The guiding Humanist principle is to do no harm to others, so each Humanist couple will work out what this means for them and how they wish to apply it to their own marriage.

SUPPORT

Humanists believe that humanity has all it needs to understand the world and that science is the best tool available to do this. They believe that, by working together, people have the sole responsibility to solve the world's problems. A key belief is 'treat others as you would be treated yourself.'

Atheists believe that there is no God. Most Humanists are also atheists.

C A civil wedding ceremony

Humanist weddings: what's the difference?

There is no set format for a Humanist wedding ceremony, and Humanist couples will often design their own. It does not have to include any particular legal wording prescribed by the state or Church. In England, Wales and Northern Ireland, Humanist wedding ceremonies are not recognised in law, but they are in Scotland. It is the person who presides over a Humanist ceremony who is licensed, not the location, so the wedding can take place anywhere.

STRETCH

Visit the British Humanist Association website to find out more about Humanist wedding celebrations.

D Humanist couples can design their own ceremony. A popular ritual is 'hand fasting', where the couple's hands are tied together by ribbons.

Christian responses

Though Christians and non-religious people may share some views on marriage, the most important difference is that Christians believe marriage is ordained by God, whereas non-religious people do not. Christian marriages are rooted in a shared belief in God and the involvement of the whole Christian community who, in a wedding ceremony, promise to support the couple in their married life.

BUILD YOUR SKILLS

1 Copy and complete the table below.

	What does it mean?	What do Christians believe about this?	What are some non-religious views on this?
Marriage			
Cohabitation			
Faithfulness			

2 'Religious understandings about marriage are outdated in today's world.' Write down arguments for and against this statement.

3 What would you include in a non-religious marriage ceremony? Explain your choices, referring to non-religious beliefs.

SUMMARY

- Marriage is an important way in which society supports couples and families.
- Christians believe in the sanctity of marriage – it is a holy gift from God.
- Many non-religious people also choose to marry, but do not believe marriage holds any religious significance.
- Many people in society choose to cohabit either before, or instead of, marrying.

EXAM-STYLE QUESTIONS

a Outline **three** Christian beliefs about marriage. (3)

b Explain **two** reasons why marriage is important to Christians. (4)

2.2 Sexual relationships

SPECIFICATION FOCUS

Christian teachings about the nature and importance of sexual relationships: divergent Christian teachings about sexual relationships; Christian attitudes towards sexual relationships outside of marriage and homosexuality, including interpretations of 1 Corinthians 6: 7–20; divergent Christian and non-religious (including atheist and Humanist) attitudes to sexual relationships, including the acceptance of sexual relationships outside marriage and homosexuality and Christian responses to them.

How does Christianity view sexual relationships?

The mainstream view within Christianity is that sex should be between a man and a woman in the context of marriage and that marriage should be for life. Married couples should be faithful to each other and therefore **promiscuity** (having sexual relations with multiple partners on a casual basis) and **adultery** (when a married person has sex with someone other than their spouse) are considered by Christians to be wrong.

> ‘You shall not commit adultery.’
> *(Exodus 20: 14)*

> ‘It is God's will that you should be sanctified: that you should avoid sexual immorality.’
> *(1 Thessalonians 4: 3)*

> ‘The sexual act must take place exclusively within marriage. Outside marriage it always constitutes a grave sin.’
> *(Catechism of the Catholic Church)*

Sex outside marriage

Most Christians believe that sex should only take place within the marriage relationship. The reasons for this incude the following:

- sex is the highest expression of love between a couple, which involves giving oneself completely to the other person in a life-long commitment
- sexual union is meant to be the consummation (end) of a loving relationship, not a precursor to it
- the Bible contains teachings about sexual relationships which uphold the sanctity of marriage (see 2.1).

However, some Christians believe that sex before marriage is acceptable if the couple love each other and they are in a long-term relationship leading to marriage.

It is important to understand that Christians do not see sex itself as wrong: they believe it is the highest expression of love between a couple. Many Christians believe, therefore, that it is right to save the gift of a sexual relationship for their future marriage partner. Choosing not to have sex before marriage is called sexual **abstinence**.

Adultery is forbidden in the Ten Commandments (*Exodus 20: 14, Leviticus 20: 10*) and this is repeated several times in the New Testament. In Ancient Israel it was punishable by death. In the UK, adultery is not a crime and cannot be punished by the law, although it is legal grounds for divorce in civil law.

A Many Christians wait until they are married before having sex with their partner

Most Christians believe that adultery is always wrong because it breaks the bond of trust between married partners and undermines the stability of family life.

Many Christians, for example Catholics, believe that remarriage after divorce amounts to adultery. This is based on teachings such as *Mark 10: 11* (see 2.6). However, other Christians believe that remarriage is acceptable under certain circumstances, for example marital unfaithfulness. This is based on teachings such as *Matthew 5: 31–32*.

Humanist beliefs about sexual relationships

Humanists aim to live good lives without being guided by religious beliefs. A Humanist, therefore, would value the freedom to have a sexual relationship when they choose to, as long as it does not cause physical or emotional harm to anyone else. If anyone would be hurt by unfaithfulness or by sexual relationships outside or before marriage, then a Humanist would consider it to be wrong, but if all parties are happy, then there are no rules to restrict them.

What is homosexuality?

Homosexuality is sexual attraction to members of one's own sex, as opposed to **heterosexuality**, which is attraction to members of the opposite sex.

In the UK, the age of consent for homosexual and heterosexual sexual activity is 16. In the past, homosexual people were shunned by society and the law did not recognise their relationships. However, the first same-sex civil partnerships took place in the UK in 2005 and same-sex marriages were conducted from 2014.

USEFUL TERMS

Abstinence: choosing to restrain oneself from doing something, for example, having sex or eating food (also called fasting)

Adultery: when a married person has a sexual relationship with someone other than their spouse

Heterosexuality: sexual attraction to members of the opposite sex

Homosexuality: sexual attraction to members of the same sex

Promiscuity: sexual relations with multiple partners on a casual basis

Christian perspectives

Views about homosexuality differ among Christians. Both the Anglican and Catholic Church have traditionally taught that homosexual activity (as distinct from feelings) falls short of the ideal expression of sexual love, which should be set within the framework of a faithful marriage between a man and a woman. These Christians would refer to Bible teachings such as the following:

‘Do not have sexual relations with a man as one does with a woman; that is detestable.’
(Leviticus 18: 22)

‘Flee from **sexual immorality**. All other sins a person commits are outside the body, but **whoever sins sexually, sins against their own body**. Do you not know that your bodies are temples of the Holy Spirit, who is in you, whom you have received from God? You are not your own; you were bought at a price. Therefore **honour God with your bodies**.’
(1 Corinthians 6: 18–20)

Other Christians interpret these passages differently, for example because they have different views about how the passages have been translated from the original languages, or because they believe the context in which the Bible was written needs to be taken into account. The Lesbian and Gay Christian Movement was founded in 1976 and in 1979 a Church of England working party said: ‘There are circumstances in which individuals may justifiably choose to enter into a homosexual relationship with the hope of enjoying companionship and a physical expression of love similar to that found in marriage’ (*Homosexual Relationships*, Church of England Board for Social Responsibility).

Most Christian denominations are in discussion about their understanding of traditional teaching and how to apply it to the modern world.

USEFUL TERMS

Pride or **Gay Pride:** a social movement encouraging homosexual people to express their sexuality openly and with self-esteem

STRETCH

1 What does the phrase ‘sexual immorality’ mean to you?

2 What might it mean to other people?

SUPPORT

Read this quote from the Church of England working party. What does this mean for homosexual Christians?

B Bishop Gene Robinson speaking at the San Francisco Pride Parade; Robinson was in an openly gay relationship when he was made a bishop in the US, despite opposition from many Christians

Lesbian and Gay Christian Movement

C The Lesbian and Gay Christian Movement logo; more information can be found on their website: **www.lgcm.org.uk**

D

Non-religious perspectives

For Humanists, same-sex relationships are fully accepted as long as the people involved consent and the relationship does not cause harm. Humanists have a strong emphasis on personal choice, including preferences in sexual orientation and behaviour. Humanist celebrants (in effect, non-religious ministers) often assist at weddings between same-sex couples.

Views among atheists on homosexuality are varied. Like Humanists, atheists do not give authority to religious teachings and therefore they are likely to accept homosexual relationships. However, some atheists – particularly older generations – may nevertheless oppose homosexuality on social or cultural grounds.

BUILD YOUR SKILLS

1 Create a spider diagram headed 'sexual relationships'.
   a Write down key Christian beliefs and teachings.
   b In another colour, explain any different Christian viewpoints.
   c In another colour, write down non-religious viewpoints.

2 Why are there different views on homosexual relationships? Write a paragraph to explain, referring to both Christian and non-religious viewpoints.

3 Read *John 8: 1–11.* What can you learn from this passage about Jesus' attitude to adultery? STRETCH

SUMMARY

- Many Christians believe that sex should take place only within marriage.
- Christian beliefs about homosexuality vary and many Christians are opposed to same-sex relationships and marriages.
- Humanists value freely chosen sexual relationships as long as they do not cause harm to others.

EXAM-STYLE QUESTIONS

a Outline **three** Christian beliefs about sex outside of marriage. (3)

c Explain **two** different Christian beliefs about homosexuality. In your answer you must refer to a source of wisdom and authority. (5)

2.3 Families

SPECIFICATION FOCUS

Christian teachings about the purpose and importance of the family including: procreation, security and education of children, with reference to Ephesians 6: 1–4; divergent Christian responses to different types of family within 21st-century society (nuclear, single parent, same-sex parents, extended and blended families).

The family unit is considered by many to be the basis of Western society. The importance of having children and raising a family is emphasised in the Christian marriage service. Christians believe that children should be brought up in a loving and supportive family environment.

Family structures

There are five family types within twenty-first-century society:

- **nuclear family** – two parents, who may be married or unmarried, and their children all living together
- **same-sex family** – two same-sex parents and their children, who may be biologically related to either of the partners
- **extended family** – parents, children and other relations such as grandparents, aunts, uncles and cousins living close together
- **single-parent family** – one parent living alone with their children; this may be due to divorce, separation, the death of the other partner or because the parent is voluntarily without a partner
- **blended family** – parents living together with children that one or both of them had in previous relationships.

While the family is valued in Christianity, different denominations have different responses to the diversity of family structures in today's society.

USEFUL TERMS

Procreation: to have sex and produce children

CASE STUDY: RESPONSES TO DIFFERENT FAMILY STRUCTURES

We uphold the biblical definition of marriage as the foundation of society and family life [...] [Nevertheless] our structures, our services and our speech should adapt to relate to people's lived experiences [...] We need to strive to have truly transgenerational worship with children, students, unmarried people and grandparents all having a part to play [...] Food banks, lone parent support, after school clubs, and help to manage family finances are just some ways in which churches can adapt their ministry to the community.
(Evangelical Magazine)

There are absolutely no grounds for considering homosexual unions to be in any way similar or even remotely analogous to God's plan for marriage and family.
(Catechism of the Catholic Church)

Families today can involve single parents, unmarried parents, parents of the same sex, adopted children, fostered children, and children born from IVF. The details of family arrangements hardly matter if they are committed to sharing resources and mutual love and support.
(British Humanist Association)

The family remains the most important grouping human beings have ever developed. Children thrive, grow and develop within the love and safeguarding of a family. Within the family we care for the young, the old and those with caring needs. Families should be able to offer each of their members commitment, fun, love, companionship and security.
(Church of England website, 'Family' page)

A A nuclear family

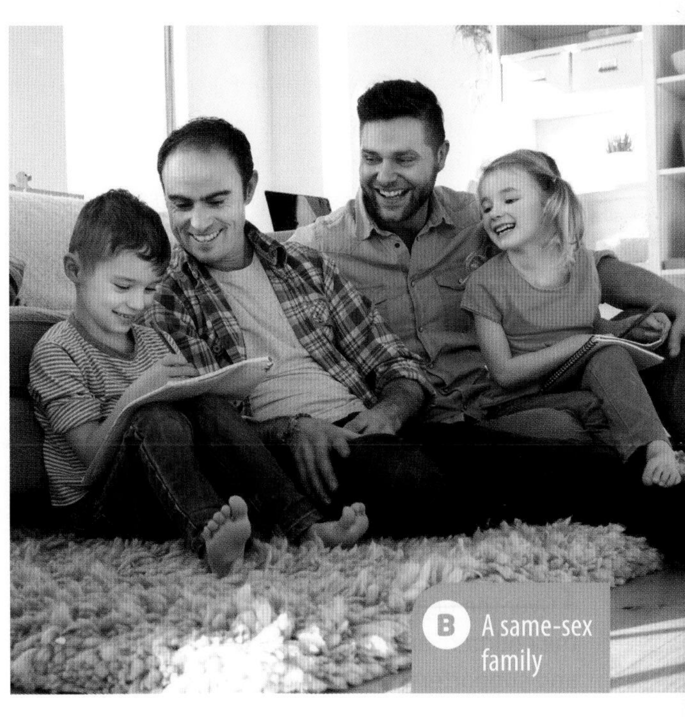

B A same-sex family

What is the purpose of the family, according to Christian teachings?

Procreation and education

Most Christians believe that one of the purposes of marriage is **procreation** and that family life is a natural goal for Christians. They believe that children are a gift from God and parents should look after them properly, providing security, medical care, food, shelter, clothing, opportunities to develop their talents and an appropriate education. The family is the setting in which children learn how to live, form relationships, and worship God.

At baptism, Christian parents will often promise to protect their child, to bring them up in a loving way, and to teach them about God. In return, children are expected to respect their parents' authority and to care for them in their own times of need.

'Honour your father and your mother.'
(Exodus 20: 12)

Christian families usually educate their children within their faith. The Church offers support for this through Sunday school and youth groups, and outreach in schools.

'Children, obey your parents [...] Fathers, do not exasperate your children; instead, **bring them up in the training and instruction of the Lord.**'
(Ephesians 6: 1, 4)

'The family is the community in which, from childhood, one can learn moral values, begin to honour God and make good use of freedom.'
(Catechism of the Catholic Church)

Give examples of how Christians might carry out this commandment today.

The security of the family

Christians believe that all children have the right to be brought up in a secure, loving family setting. Many Christians support charities involved with family life, for example The Children's Society, which works with the Church of England and others to support vulnerable children, and Action for Children, which has an active partnership with the Methodist Church and helps families and children in care.

> ‘Our charity was founded in 1881 by Edward Rudolf, a Sunday School teacher, and our partnership with the Church has been of central importance ever since. We want to work in partnership with every single parish in the Church of England [...] We would like to work with all people who share our values, whether Christians from other denominations, people of all faiths and none.’
> *(The Children's Society website)*

> ‘Over the years, Stephenson's commitment to his work ‘in the service of the children’ and Methodist principles have been an inspiration to our staff and supporters. Our work has evolved from just running children's homes to providing wide-ranging services that match the modern challenges of disadvantaged children, young people and families.’
> *(Action for Children website)*

The Children's Society

C The Children's Society supports children experiencing poverty and neglect

BUILD YOUR SKILLS

1. Write down each of the five types of family and explain each one.
2. What is the purpose of family for Christians? Write a paragraph to explain.
3. Which types of family might some Christians disagree with? Explain why, using 2.1 and 2.2 to help you.

SUMMARY

- There are five family types within twenty-first-century society.
- Many Christians believe that an important purpose of marriage is to have children.
- Charities like The Children's Society work in partnership with the Church to support vulnerable children and their families.

EXAM-STYLE QUESTIONS

a. Outline **three** different family types in twenty-first-century society. (3)

d. ‘Children need to be brought up in secure family units.’ Evaluate this statement considering arguments for and against. In your response you should:
   - refer to Christian teachings
   - reach a justified conclusion. (12)

2.4 Support for the family in the local parish

SPECIFICATION FOCUS

Support for the family in the local parish: how and why the local church community tries to support families, including through family worship, including interpretations of Matthew 19: 13–14, rites of passage, classes for parents, groups for children, including Sunday schools and counselling; the importance of the support of the local parish for Christians today.

How do parishes support families?

The Christian understanding of the importance of children can be drawn from various Bible passages, but possibly the most well-known is found in *Matthew 19: 13–14*, in which people bring their children to Jesus to be prayed for, but the disciples try to send them away. It appears that the disciples didn't think children important enough to come to Jesus, but Jesus says: 'Let the little children come to me, and do not hinder them, for the kingdom of heaven belongs to such as these.'

From Bible verses such as *Matthew 19: 14* churches see children as having an important position within the faith community, and try to help parents raise their children in a stable, Christian environment. When they are older, the children can choose to take the baptismal vows themselves, in a believer's baptism or confirmation (see 3.2). As the children grow up, they can learn about God in their family, but also in their Sunday schools (church children's groups) and church youth groups. Catholic, Anglican and denominational church schools can complement this by offering education in a Christian environment.

Churches may support families in different ways:

- holding family services on Sundays and special events in the church year
- supporting organisations such as Scouts and Brownies
- operating food banks
- running courses on parenting, money, depression and so on
- offering counselling through organisations such as the Catholic Marriage Advisory Council and the Child Welfare Council
- helping Christian adults to look after elderly parents through such organisations as the Methodist Homes for the Aged
- offering practical support for families in the UK and around the world through organisations such as the Mothers' Union.

Family worship

A typical service of family worship may include:

- a welcoming atmosphere for children
- a section which is targeted at children, such as a short talk
- time during the service when children have separate Sunday school activities
- a time during the service in which children participate, for example, they may show what they have done during Sunday school
- inclusion of children in running the service, as servers or in a choir
- opportunities for teenagers to lead worship.

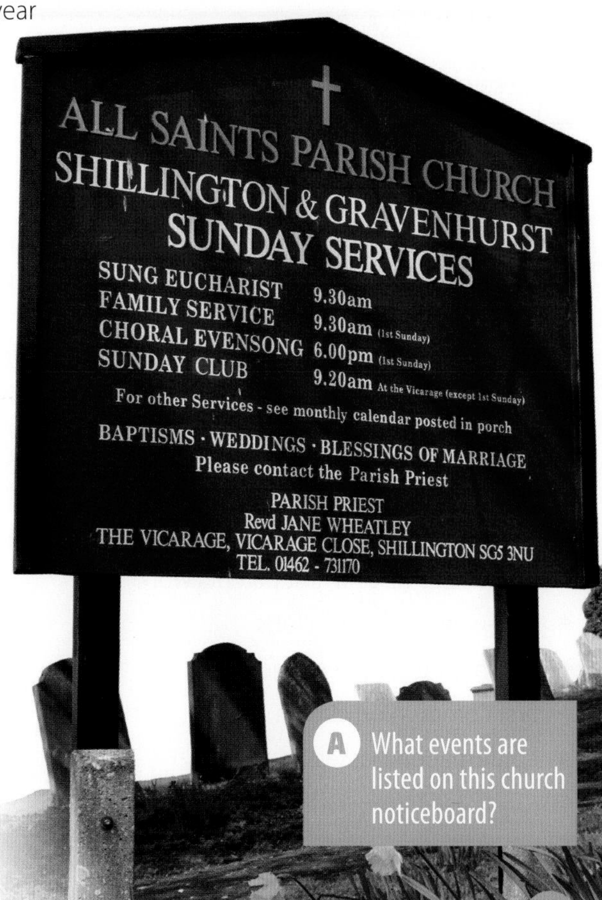

A What events are listed on this church noticeboard?

Some churches offer services at particular times of the year especially with children in mind, for example:

- **Christingle** events
- Christmas Eve crib service
- Mothering Sunday service
- harvest festival
- animal blessing services.

Involving children in worship in this way includes children in church life from an early stage. Their parents may find it easier to continue to attend church and to draw on support from the church community. As children grow up they may be more likely to have an interest in Christianity, and continue to participate in the church in the future.

B A flier for a church's 'kids club'; do you think clubs like this would appeal to local families?

Rites of passage

Rites of passage are special events which show that a person is moving on to a new stage in life. The Church supports many rites of passage when family members and friends come to church, and for children they include:

- baptism or christenings
- thanksgiving services for the birth of a baby and welcoming them into the Church
- preparation for first communion or confirmation
- confirmation services.

These services have different meanings for different churches but all focus on welcoming and including children.

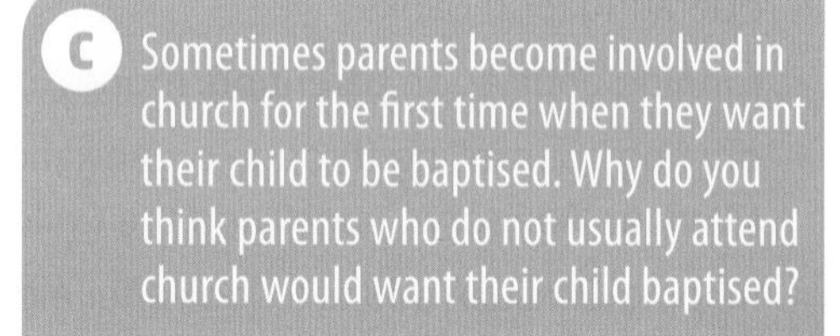

C Sometimes parents become involved in church for the first time when they want their child to be baptised. Why do you think parents who do not usually attend church would want their child baptised?

Groups for children and parents

Churches don't just operate on Sundays. As well as offering Sunday schools for children, during the week many churches have a full programme of events to include children, including:

- parent and baby or toddler groups
- music, art and drama classes for children
- tuition classes to support school work for older children
- school assemblies
- hosting childcare groups that run from church premises whilst parents work
- mid-week children's clubs
- youth groups for teenagers
- first communion classes
- confirmation classes.

Groups aimed at parents might include:

- parenting classes
- family counselling and practical help from qualified therapists and professionals
- marriage enrichment groups
- baptism preparation classes (for those wanting their children baptised and people becoming godparents)
- Mothers' Union support in areas such as literacy, bereavement, poverty and imprisonment.

Church groups aimed at adults (not just those with children) include:

- Alpha courses for those exploring the Christian faith
- social events – barbecues, barn dances, quiz nights, carnivals and so on
- clubs and outings for older people
- coffee mornings
- Bible study discussion groups.

Local parish support

As well as supporting the church community, local churches are often active in the wider parish, with outreach activities such as:

- visiting people who are sick, lonely or isolated at home
- visiting people in hospital
- visiting people who are in prison or other difficult circumstances.

USEFUL TERMS

Christingle: a lighted candle symbolising Jesus as the light of the world, often carried by children in church celebrations around Christmas time

Rites of passage: events marking key stages in life

BUILD YOUR SKILLS

1 Which of the following statements, if any, do you agree with? Explain why.
   - 'Without children the Church has no relevance in society.'
   - 'The Church should include children and young people much more.'
   - 'Christianity is fine for families with children, but they will grow out of it when they are older.'

2 Look up the websites of three local churches and find out what they offer for children and families. In pairs or small groups make a short presentation on their programmes and explain how these events comply with *Matthew 19: 13–14*.

SUMMARY

- Churches work to support families in raising their children in a Christian environment.
- Family worship encourages families to include their children in church activities.
- Rites of passage enable children to become part of the Church as they grow up.
- Many churches offer family support outside of worship on a Sunday.

EXAM-STYLE QUESTIONS

a Outline **three** ways that the local church supports parents. (3)

c Explain **two** reasons why supporting families is important to Christians. In your answer you must refer to a source of wisdom and authority. (5)

2.5 Contraception

What is family planning?

Family planning means choosing when to have children, by using **contraception** (artificial or natural methods) to regulate births.

Family planning involves using one of a number of methods to prevent pregnancy. Artificial methods include the contraceptive pill, condoms, and the IUD (coil). An example of a natural method is the rhythm method (planning sex around the times in the woman's menstrual cycle when she is least likely to conceive) or, most radically, sterilisation or vasectomy.

Christian teachings

Religious believers have different views about the use of contraception. Christian acceptance of artificial methods of contraception is relatively new since all churches disapproved of it until the early twentieth century. Anglicans were the first to speak out in favour of artificial contraception at the Lambeth Conference in 1930.

The Catholic Church and some Protestant churches are traditionally the most conservative on the subject, believing that artificial contraception is a sinful act since it prevents humans from fulfilling God's command to 'Be fruitful and increase in number' *(Genesis 1: 28)*.

> So God created mankind in his own image, in the image of God he created them; male and female he created them. God blessed them and said to them, '**Be fruitful and increase in number**; fill the earth and subdue it.'
> *(Genesis 1: 27–28)*

Christians who adopt this view believe that every act of sexual intercourse should be open to the possibility of **conception** and people should only use a natural method of birth control such as the rhythm method. Some conservative Christians will not even agree with this approach and argue that a couple should never deliberately avoid the possibility of pregnancy.

Catholic churches refer to the important encyclical letter *Humanae Vitae* (Latin for 'human life') issued by Pope Paul VI in 1968 which confirmed the Church's traditional teaching that it is wrong to use artificial contraception to prevent new human beings from coming into existence. Official Catholic teaching is that use of artificial contraception is a grave sin and that it should never be considered.

This is out of respect for God as the ultimate source of life:

> ...to experience the gift of married love while respecting the laws of conception is to acknowledge that one is not the master of the sources of life but rather the minister of the design established by the Creator.
> *(Humanae Vitae, II.13)*

SPECIFICATION FOCUS

Christian teaching about family planning and regulation of births: divergent Christian attitudes about contraception and family planning, including teachings about the artificial methods of contraception by some Protestant Churches and the Catholic Church, with reference to Humanae Vitae; different non-religious (including atheist and Humanist) attitudes to family planning and the application of ethical theories such as situation ethics and Christian responses to them.

USEFUL TERMS

Conception: the moment when a sperm fertilises an egg, creating an embryo that can develop into a baby

Contraception: artificial and natural methods of preventing pregnancy; also known as birth control

STRETCH

Christians who are opposed to contraception also use this teaching from *Psalm 127: 3–5*. What do you think?

> Children are a heritage from the Lord, offspring a reward from him. Like arrows in the hands of a warrior are children born in one's youth. Blessed is the man whose quiver is full of them.

The different methods of contraception are also controversial and Christians have different views about them.

Method	How it works	Christian views
Cap or condom used with spermicides	Acts as a barrier to prevent conception	Strictest would reject, but others accept as it acts before conception takes place
The contraceptive pill, injection or patch	A chemical barrier to prevent conception	Strictest would reject, but others accept as it acts before conception takes place
IUD or coil	Prevents a fertilised egg from implanting in the womb	Some Christians may reject as conception has already taken place
Morning-after pill	A chemical method to prevent a fertilised egg from implanting	Most Christians may reject as conception has already taken place, but also because it may encourage irresponsible sexual behaviour since it does not require any consideration before having sex
Sterilisation or vasectomy	A surgical procedure making it impossible to conceive	Strictest would reject; some may accept on health grounds, or if a couple decide not to have any more children

Non-religious attitudes to family planning

Humanists believe that people should think for themselves and make decisions based on human well-being, not on what religious teachings say. Most Humanists have no ethical objections to birth control, arguing that *if* contraception 'results in every child being a wanted child, and in better, healthier lives for women, it must be a good thing' (British Humanist Association). Most Humanists assess the rights and wrongs of contraception by looking at the consequences of birth control and say that if contraception leads to good results it is ethically right to use it.

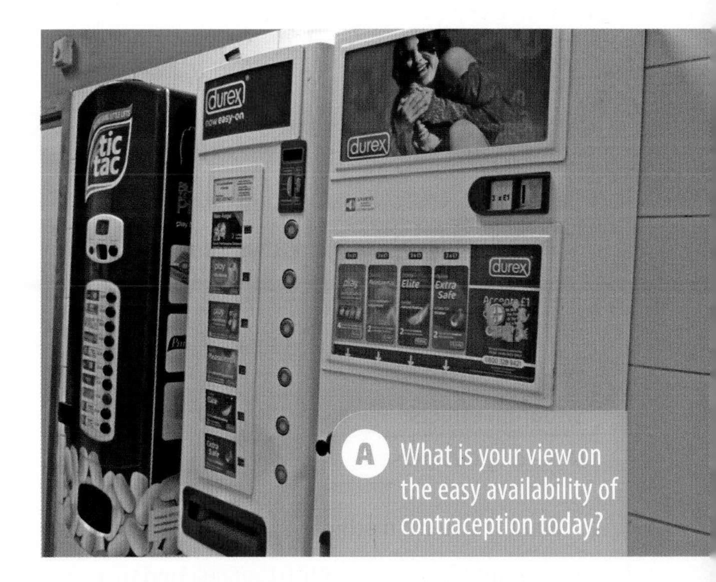

A What is your view on the easy availability of contraception today?

In the past, non-religious views clashed significantly with the position held by Christians. For example, in 1877 Charles Bradlaugh, leader of the National Secular Society, and his partner Annie Besant, were given prison sentences for publishing a book that supported contraception. The Church's perspective at the time was that people should not be interfering with nature. The Humanist response today is that it is not wrong to interfere with nature if the consequences are positive for all involved.

The twenty-first-century Church does still have denominations which see artificial contraception as being wrong. However, on the whole other Protestant and liberal Christians tend to be in agreement with the Humanists and adopt more flexible approaches; they consider that within a marriage relationship contraception can be used responsibly to plan and manage a family.

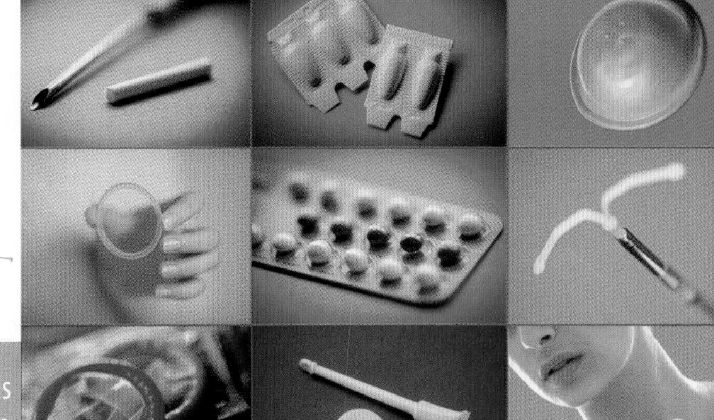
B Can you identify these different methods of contraception? Which are more or less acceptable to different Christian groups?

Making ethical choices

Some ethical theories adopt a particular principle or rule when making moral decisions. **Situation ethics** is an ethical theory first suggested by an American scholar called Joseph Fletcher. Situation ethics says that the only rule that should be followed is: in any situation do the most loving action. This is why it is called *situation* ethics.

C

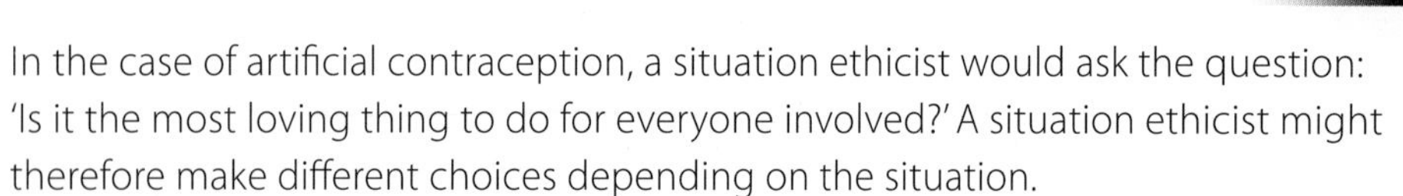

In the case of artificial contraception, a situation ethicist would ask the question: 'Is it the most loving thing to do for everyone involved?' A situation ethicist might therefore make different choices depending on the situation.

In contrast to this, most Christians make decisions based on the Bible, the teachings of the Church, and their own conscience. Whilst many Christians would respond to situations (as in, for example, the use of artificial contraception) with a degree of flexibility, others, for example Catholic Christians, would apply one rule to all situations.

STRETCH

How would a Catholic, a liberal Christian, a Humanist, and a situation ethicist respond to the following two scenarios?

- A couple decide they are not yet ready to have children and will use the coil as a method of contraception.
- A couple decide they don't want to have children and so they decide to have an operation to ensure they don't get pregnant.

BUILD YOUR SKILLS

1 Complete the table below:

	Views about contraception	Arguments for and against this view
Catholic Christian		
Liberal Christian		
Situation ethicist		
Non-religious person		

2 What is situation ethics? Explain the theory in your own words.

3 How would a Catholic Christian respond to a situation ethicist on the subject of using artificial contraception? Write a paragraph in answer to this question, referring to *Humanae Vitae*.

USEFUL TERMS

Situation ethics: ethical decisions made according to the specific context of the decision

SUMMARY

- Catholic Christians reject the use of artificial contraception but accept natural methods, whereas some more conservative Christians reject all forms of contraception as being against God's plan for humans to have children.
- More liberal Christians will accept the use of artificial contraception, but some may reject certain types, for instance the morning-after pill.
- Humanists believe that contraception should be considered in relation to whether or not it harms anyone.

EXAM-STYLE QUESTIONS

b Explain **two** different Christian beliefs about contraception. (4)

d 'People should decide for themselves what contraception they use.' Evaluate this statement considering arguments for and against. In your response you should:

- refer to Christian teachings
- refer to different Christian points of view
- refer to non-religious points of view
- refer to relevant ethical arguments
- reach a justified conclusion. (12)

2.6 Divorce

SPECIFICATION FOCUS

Christian teachings and attitudes towards divorce and remarriage: Christian teachings about divorce and remarriage, including Matthew 19: 1–12; divergent Christian, non-religious (including atheist and Humanist) attitudes to divorce and remarriage, including the application of ethical theories, such as situation ethics, and Christian responses to them.

What is divorce?

A divorce is the legal termination of a marriage. UK law allows divorce if a marriage has 'irretrievably broken down'. The most common reasons are adultery, unreasonable behaviour and desertion.

- There were 114,720 divorces in England and Wales in 2013, a decrease of 2.9 per cent since 2012, when there were 118,140 divorces.
- In 2013, there were 9.8 divorces per thousand married couples, and divorce was highest among couples aged 40 to 44.
- For those married in 1968, 20 per cent of marriages had ended in divorce by the 15th wedding anniversary whereas for those who married in 1998, almost a third of marriages (32 per cent) had ended within 15 years.

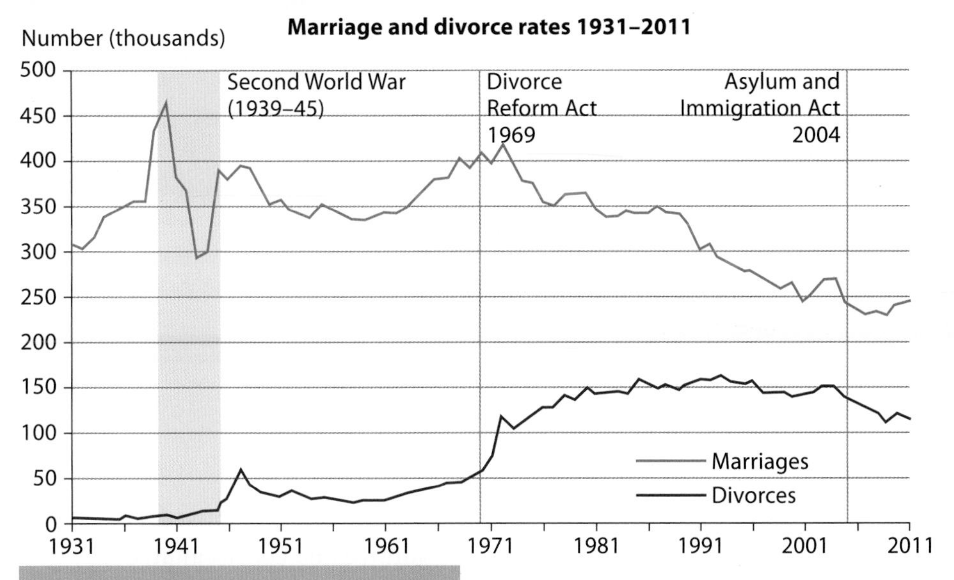

A How have marriage and divorce rates changed over this 80-year period?

B The Duke of Windsor, formerly Edward VIII, with Mrs Wallis Simpson, 1937

Divorce was once not socially acceptable. However, today, things are different:

- Divorce is easier and cheaper to obtain than it was even 40 years ago.
- People are less prepared to put up with bad treatment from their partners.
- Divorced people are not discriminated against in society.

Those who oppose divorce argue that it is the easy way out of marital difficulties and people should try harder to solve problems, especially if they have children.

Those who support divorce see it as a compassionate law that frees people from a relationship which has broken down.

In 1936 Edward VIII withdrew as king in order to marry a divorced woman. In 2005 Prince Charles married divorcee Camilla Parker-Bowles with no question over his eligibility to become king. How does this reflect changes in society?

C Prince Charles and Camilla Parker-Bowles, after their civil wedding ceremony, 2005

What are the Christian teachings on divorce and remarriage?

The wedding ceremony in the Church of England Service Book says: 'That which God has joined together, let no one divide', underlining the ideal of marriage as a lifelong union. The Christian Church is divided on the subject of divorce. The problem stems from the fact that, in the Bible, Jesus appears to give two different teachings.

In Mark's Gospel, Jesus appears to forbid divorce: 'Anyone who divorces his wife and marries another woman commits adultery against her' *(Mark 10: 11)*. However, in Matthew's Gospel, Jesus appears to allow for divorce in the case of unfaithfulness:

> '... they are no longer two, but one flesh. Therefore what God has joined together, let no one separate. 'Why then,' they asked, 'did Moses command that a man give his wife a certificate of divorce and send her away?' Jesus replied, 'Moses permitted you to divorce your wives because your hearts were hard. But it was not this way from the beginning. I tell you that **anyone who divorces his wife, except for sexual immorality, and marries another woman commits adultery.**'
> *(Matthew 19: 6–9)*

D Why might Christians be concerned about the idea expressed in this picture?

In *1 Corinthians 7: 10–11* Paul writes: 'To the married I give this command (not I, but the Lord): A wife must not separate from her husband. But if she does, she must remain unmarried or else be reconciled to her husband. And a husband must not divorce his wife.'

The Catholic view

The Catholic Church does not believe divorce is possible because the marriage vows are a covenant (agreement), made by both partners to each other and to God. Therefore, they claim, a couple can never be divorced according to God's law. A Catholic who does divorce cannot remarry in a Catholic church.

However, the Catholic Church will declare a marriage to be null (known as annulment – see 2.1) in certain particular circumstances, for example the couple being forced to marry or being under age.

> 'Between the baptised, a ratified and consummated marriage cannot be dissolved by any human power or for any reason other than death.'
> *(Catechism of the Catholic Church, 2382)*

The Protestant view

In the mainstream Protestant Church, divorce can be permitted on the grounds that:

- human beings make mistakes and relationships do break down
- God forgives mistakes
- after asking God's forgiveness, therefore, believers may divorce and marry again.

Divorced people can remarry in a Protestant church if the local clergy agree to it; otherwise their marriage may be blessed. However, conservative Protestants still disapprove of divorce and remarriage.

> 'Marriage should always be undertaken as a lifelong commitment but there are circumstances in which a divorced person may be married in church.'
> *(Church of England statement on marriage)*

What are some non-religious views?

Non-religious views are also varied on the subject of divorce. Some atheists may object to divorce, but this will be because of social or cultural reasons, not religious ones. Others will argue that it is up to the couple to decide what is best for them. This latter view is shared by Humanists:

> 'Though marriage is a useful social institution, humanists do not believe that it is 'sacred', recognise that some relationships fail, and so support liberal divorce laws.'
> *(Family Matters, British Humanist Association)*

Should elaborate weddings be avoided, since many marriages do not last?

BUILD YOUR SKILLS

1. What do the following words mean? Divorce, remarriage, annulment
2. Why do Christians disagree about divorce and remarriage? Refer to Christian teachings.
3. Remind yourself about situation ethics (see 2.5) and answer the following:
   a. In what situation would a situation ethicist argue *for* divorce, and in what situation would they argue *against* it? Outline two scenarios and explain your reasoning.
   b. How would a Christian respond to these arguments and why?
4. Describe what annulment is and some of the reasons why it is allowed. **STRETCH**

SUMMARY

- Divorce is the legal termination of a marriage. Divorce is readily available in the twenty-first century but the rate is now slowing down.
- Catholics may have their marriages annulled but may not divorce.
- Protestants may allow divorcees to remarry in church.
- Humanists believe divorce can reduce unhappiness.

EXAM-STYLE QUESTIONS

a. Outline **three** Christian teachings about divorce. (3)

d. 'Christians should be more understanding when marriages break down.'
Evaluate this statement considering arguments for and against. In your response you should:
- refer to Christian teachings
- refer to different Christian points of view
- refer to non-religious points of view
- reach a justified conclusion.
(12)

2.7 Equality of men and women in the family

What are Christian teachings about the equality of men and women?

Most Christians believe that men and women are equal, which is based on the biblical teaching that both men and women were created in the image of God. In the creation account of *Genesis 1*, men and women are created at the same time, and both are given authority to rule over the rest of creation:

> 'Then God said, 'Let us make mankind in our image, in our likeness, so that they may rule over the fish in the sea and the birds in the sky, over the livestock and all the wild animals, and over all the creatures that move along the ground.' **So God created mankind in his own image, in the image of God he created them; male and female he created them.**'
> *(Genesis 1: 26–27)*

In the *Genesis 2* account, men and women are created separately, and some Christians therefore infer that the man is superior, as he was created first and the woman is created as a companion for him.

> 'The Lord God said, '**It is not good for the man to be alone. I will make a helper suitable for him**' [...] So [...] he took one of the man's ribs and then closed up the place with flesh. Then the Lord God made a woman from the rib he had taken out of the man, and he brought her to the man. The man said, 'This is now bone of my bones and flesh of my flesh; she shall be called 'woman,' for she was taken out of man.' That is why a man leaves his father and mother and is united to his wife, and they become one flesh.'
> *(Genesis 2: 18, 21–23)*

SPECIFICATION FOCUS

Christian teaching about the equality of men and women in the family: Christian teachings and attitudes about the role of men and women in the family, including reference to Genesis 1–3 and Ephesians 5: 21–30; divergent Christian attitudes about the equality and role of men and women in the family and Christian responses to them.

USEFUL TERM

Equality: treating people in the same way irrespective of differences such as sex, race, education, disability or sexuality

A Stained glass window showing Adam, Eve, and the serpent

In *Genesis 3* the woman appears to encourage the man to disobey God's instruction not to eat from the Tree of the Knowledge of Good and Evil. Historically, some Christians have viewed women as being inferior to men on the grounds that all women share the blame for tempting the man.

In *Genesis 3: 16* the woman is punished for her role in tempting the man to disobey God, leading some Christians to suggest that pain in childbirth and male domination within marriage would not otherwise have happened.

> 'I will make your pains in childbearing very severe; with painful labour you will give birth to children. Your desire will be for your husband, and he will rule over you.'
> *(Genesis 3: 16)*

In the Old Testament, however, women seem to have leading roles in society and the Ten Commandments require respect for both parents equally: 'Honour your father and your mother, so that you may live long in the land the Lord your God is giving you' *(Exodus 20: 12)*. Similarly, Paul writes that Jesus teaches: 'There is neither Jew nor Gentile, neither slave nor free, nor is there male and female, for you are all one in Christ Jesus' (*Galatians 3: 28)*. Most Christians therefore believe that men and women have equal worth in God's eyes.

Another Christian teaching is that men and women are equal but different. Many Christians believe that men and women are equally valuable in the eyes of God, but that they have been given different roles by him. For example, the following teaching suggests that husbands and wives have different roles within a marriage:

> '**Wives, submit yourselves to your own husbands as you do to the Lord. For the husband is the head of the wife as Christ is the head of the church**, his body, of which he is the Saviour. [...] Husbands, love your wives, just as Christ loved the church [...] In this same way, husbands ought to love their wives as their own bodies. He who loves his wife loves himself. After all, no one ever hated their own body, but they feed and care for their body, just as Christ does the church – for we are members of his body [...] each one of you also must love his wife as he loves himself, and the wife must respect her husband.'
> *(Ephesians 5: 22–33)*

Christians who adopt this teaching in their marriages highlight the comparison to Jesus and the Church – Jesus laid down his life for the Church, and therefore the husband has the responsibility to love and protect the family. Women in turn have a responsibility to love, submit to, and respect their husbands. Some more liberal Christians do not agree that the husband is the head of the wife, and believe that both partners should submit to each other.

B Christian husbands are commanded to love their wives as much as themselves

SUPPORT

Submitting to someone else means accepting their authority or leadership. This quotation says that wives should submit to their husbands, and husbands should love their wives.

How do Christians view gender equality?

Christian denominations and Christian organisations around them have expressed a range of views on gender **equality**.

Gender equality

The Catholic Church

'The Church has the duty to contribute to the recognition and liberation of women, following the example of Christ's own esteem for them [...] Giving women opportunities [...] would enable them to occupy a place in society equal to that of men – without confusing or conflating the specific character of each – since both men and women are the 'image' of the Creator.'

(Pope Benedict XVI, Africae Munis 57, 2011)

Church of England – principles

- Belief in God as love expressed in relationships.
- Understanding of humanity (female and male) as made in God's image, and possessing equal worth.
- Equality amongst people and within relationships.

Methodist Church

'... the model of relationship between husband and wife which gives 'headship' as the responsibility of the husband and submission as the wife's part has led in many circumstances to unequal and inappropriate relationships of domination and subordination [...] being encouraged to be themselves rather than sticking to gendered roles offers a better interpretation of love and a better opportunity for both partners to grow and flourish in the relationship ...'

Mothers' Union

'Mothers' Union has gender equality as a core focus of its work. As Christians we believe that women and men are equal in the eyes of God. But [...] we see women and girls treated unequally. Too often women's contributions to family life, the workplace, the church and political life are either ignored or dismissed.'

BUILD YOUR SKILLS

1. Make a list of the different Christian views on equality of men and women.
2. Which of the following statements, if any, do you agree with? Explain why.
   - 'Women should not be given different family roles from men.'
   - 'Men and women are different. That's why they have different roles.'
   - 'In today's society we do not need to turn to ancient texts to understand gender roles in the family.'
3. Do you think men and women have equality in family life today? Explain your reasons.

SUMMARY

- Christian views on the equality of men and women are based on teachings in Genesis and in the New Testament.
- Paul teaches that the husband is the head of the wife, that wives should submit to their husbands and that husbands should love their wives.
- Many Christians interpret this to mean men and women are equal but with different roles to play. Other Christians disagree.

EXAM-STYLE QUESTIONS

a. Outline **three** Christian teachings about the equality of men and women in the family. (3)

c. Explain **two** reasons why Christians have different views about the equality of men and women in the family. In your answer you must refer to a source of wisdom and authority. (5)

2.8 Gender prejudice and discrimination

What is gender prejudice and discrimination?

Prejudice means having an opinion that is based on a preconceived idea, rather than actual experience. Discrimination means acting unfairly towards a person, on the basis of a prejudiced opinion.

There are many examples of **gender prejudice** and **gender discrimination** throughout history. For example, in the UK, women have not always had the same opportunities as men to own money and property. Until the Married Women's Property Act was passed in 1882, married women had no legal identity, and their money and possessions automatically passed to her husband when they married. Women were not able to inherit in their own right until 1922.

In more recent times, legislation such as the Sex Discrimination Act and the Equality Act have tried to prevent discrimination from occurring, but many people feel that gender prejudice and discrimination are still common in society today.

When women and men are treated differently, it is often on the basis of a gender stereotype. A stereotype is a generalised idea of supposedly typical features that something or someone may have. Generalisations can sometimes be useful, but they can also be misleading, and may not relate to the actual individual characteristics of a person at all. When people make stereotyped assumptions about others, this can lead to prejudice and discrimination.

What does Christianity teach about opposing gender prejudice and discrimination?

In *Galations*, Paul teaches Christians to regard each other as equal, in a text that is often used to encourage Christians to challenge inequality, prejudice, and discrimination of different kinds:

> '... in Christ Jesus you are all children of God through faith, for all of you who were baptised into Christ have clothed yourselves with Christ. **There is neither Jew nor Gentile, neither slave nor free, nor is there male and female, for you are all one in Christ Jesus**. If you belong to Christ, then you are Abraham's seed, and heirs according to the promise.'
> *(Galations 3: 26–29)*

SPECIFICATION FOCUS

Christian teachings about gender prejudice and discrimination: Christian opposition to gender prejudice and discrimination including Galatians 3: 23–29; examples of Christian opposition to gender prejudice and discrimination; divergent Christian attitudes to gender differences, including the role of women in the Church, prejudice and discrimination and Christian responses to them.

SUPPORT

Read this list of **gender stereotypes**. Are there any others you could add?

Gender stereotypes	
Women	**Men**
gentle	tough
emotional	rational
compassionate	assertive
weak	strong

A How does this graffiti image challenge gender stereotyping?

According to the Bible, Jesus treated men and women with equal respect. He had devoted female followers who stayed throughout his ministry, received serious teaching from him, and were there at his death and resurrection. Female followers are presented by the gospel writers in a positive light.

- Jesus healed a sick woman who was outcast from her community *(Mark 5: 24–34)*.
- He spoke to a Samaritan woman who was despised by others *(John 4: 7–27)*.
- He defended the woman who had used expensive perfume to anoint him *(Mark 14: 1–9)*.

USEFUL TERMS

Gender discrimination: acting upon prejudice about someone's gender; for example, not appointing a woman to a high-pressure job on the assumption that she must be too fragile for the role; or expecting a man to do a heavy physical task on the assumption that he must be strong

Gender prejudice: making judgements about men or women on the basis of their gender; for example, judging all women to be emotionally fragile or all men to be emotionally strong

Ordination: the appointment of men and women to professional ministry in the Church

How have Christians opposed gender prejudice and discrimination?

Most denominations in the modern Christian Church have tried to reflect Jesus' attitude towards women in different areas of life.

Wedding vows

For many years, in the Anglican wedding ceremony men vowed to 'love and cherish' their wife, while women vowed to 'love, cherish and obey' their husband. In 2006, the Church issued a report on how it could help to tackle issues of domestic violence, in which it recognised that the traditional vow of obedience could appear to condone abusive relationships. It went on to launch guidelines on acceptable alternative vows that left out the word 'obey'.

In the Methodist marriage ceremony, the word 'obey' had been dropped in the 1930s, and the practice of 'giving away' the bride was optional. The Catholic wedding service has identical forms of wording for the vows made by women and men.

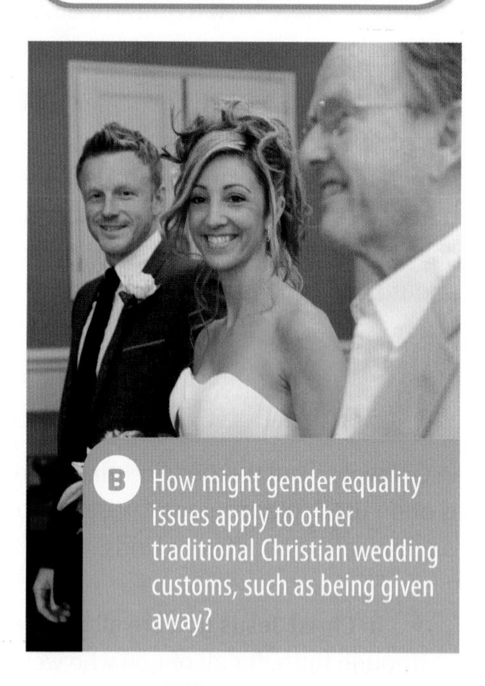

B How might gender equality issues apply to other traditional Christian wedding customs, such as being given away?

The role of women in the Church

One of the recent acts of opposition to gender discrimination in the Church of England has been the **ordination** of women into the priesthood. Some denominations have been ordaining women into the ministry for many years, but women were not permitted to become priests in the Anglican Church until 1994. The Catholic Church does not ordain women.

Those who object to the ordination of women often refer to the teaching of Paul: 'I do not permit a woman to teach or to assume authority over a man' *(1 Timothy 2: 12)*. Other arguments against women's ordination include the fact that Jesus chose only men to be the twelve disciples, and women are not given authority by God to be leaders in the Church.

Christians who are in favour of having women as ordained ministers often argue that it is not just an issue of equality and that it is good to have men and women in the priesthood because:

- women have different skills to offer their congregations
- many women are able to deal sensitively with pastoral issues
- women priests can relate better to women in the Church.

'The Lord Jesus chose men to form the twelve apostles and the apostles did the same when they chose their successors [...] For this reason the ordination of women is not possible.'
(Catechism of the Catholic Church, 1577)

C England's first women priests leave Bristol Cathedral after their ordination on 12 March, 1994

D Catholic campaigns calling for the ordination of women

After much debate, the Church of England approved the ordination of women as bishops in November 2014 and the Right Reverend Libby Lane (see image **E**) was appointed Bishop of Stockport soon after. Not all members of the Church of England agreed with this appointment, however.

BUILD YOUR SKILLS

1. Explain the following three terms: gender prejudice, gender discrimination, gender stereotype.
2. Make a bullet-pointed list which summarises the Christian teachings on gender prejudice and discrimination.
3. How do Christians oppose gender prejudice and discrimination? Describe one example.
4. Why do you think Christians disagree over the role of women in the Church? Explain your views, referring to Christian teachings.

SUMMARY

- Gender prejudice and discrimination is illegal in the UK, but is still experienced by many.
- Jesus treated men and women with equal respect and included women in his ministry.
- Women were first ordained in the Church of England in 1994 and the first female bishop was ordained in 2014. The Catholic Church does not ordain women.

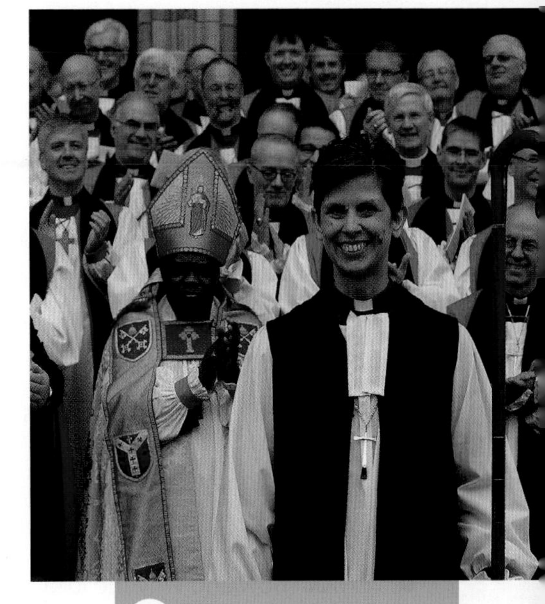

E Libby Lane, the first female Church of England bishop

EXAM-STYLE QUESTIONS

b Explain **two** reasons why some Christians oppose the ordination of women. (4)

d 'Women should have the same leadership roles as men within the Church.' Evaluate this statement considering arguments for and against. In your response you should:
- refer to Christian teachings
- refer to different Christian points of view
- reach a justified conclusion. (12)

Revision

BUILD YOUR SKILLS

Look at the list of 'I can' statements below and think carefully about how confident you are. Use the following code to rate each of the statements. Be honest!

Green – very confident. What is your evidence for this?

Orange – quite confident. What is your target? Be specific.

Red – not confident. What is your target? Be specific.

A self-assessment revision checklist is available on *Kerboodle*

I can…

- Give Christian teachings about marriage
- Explain the purpose and importance of marriage for Christians
- Explain different views about the importance of marriage in society, including non-religious views, and Christian responses to them
- Give Christian teachings about sexual relationships
- Explain different Christian attitudes towards relationships outside of marriage
- Explain different Christian attitudes towards homosexuality
- Explain non-religious views about sexual relationships and Christian responses to them
- Give Christian teachings about the purpose and importance of family
- Describe the five different types of family within twenty-first-century society
- Explain different Christian responses to different types of family
- Explain how and why the local church community tries to support families, with reference to a source of wisdom and authority
- Describe the various activities organised by churches today for families
- Give Christian teachings about family planning and regulation of births
- Explain different Christian attitudes about contraception and family planning, including Protestant and Catholic attitudes, with reference to *Humanae Vitae*
- Explain different non-religious attitudes about contraception and family planning and Christian responses to them
- Apply situation ethics to issues surrounding contraception and explain how Christians would respond
- Give Christian teachings about divorce and remarriage
- Explain different Christian attitudes about divorce and remarriage
- Explain different non-religious attitudes about divorce and remarriage and Christian responses to them
- Apply situation ethics to issues surrounding divorce and remarriage and explain how Christians would respond
- Give Christian teachings about the equality of men and women in the family
- Explain different Christian views about the roles of men and women in the family
- Give Christian teachings about gender prejudice and discrimination
- Give examples of how Christians have opposed gender prejudice and discrimination
- Explain different Christian attitudes to gender differences, including the role of women in the Church.

Exam practice

On these exam practice pages you will see example answers for each of the exam question types: **a**, **b**, **c**, and **d**. You can find out more about these on pages 6–11.

• Question 'a'

*Question **a** is AO1 – this tests your knowledge and understanding.*

(a) Outline **three** Christian beliefs about marriage. (3)

Student response

Marriage is one flesh, married people can't get divorced, married people should be faithful to each other.

Improved student response

Christians believe that when they get married they become 'one flesh'. Some Christians, for example Catholics, believe that you can't get divorced once you are married in the eyes of God. Christians believe married people should be faithful to each other.

Over to you! Give yourself three minutes on the clock and have a go at answering this question. Remember, this question type requires you to provide three facts or short ideas: you don't need to explain them.

WHAT WENT WELL

The student has touched on some key Christian ideas – for example the importance of faithfulness. The student has attempted to give three different Christian beliefs.

HOW TO IMPROVE

A little more detail is required to ensure that the points reflect Christian beliefs more fully, and to allow for the diverse views within Christianity. See the 'improved student response' opposite for suggested corrections.

• Question 'b'

*Question **b** is AO1 – this tests your knowledge and understanding.*

(b) Explain **two** different Christian beliefs about contraception. (4)

Student response

Many Christians believe that you shouldn't use contraception because God told Adam and Eve to fill the earth. These Christians think that only God can create life and decide who should and should not get pregnant.

Improved student response

Many Christians, for example Catholics, believe that you shouldn't use artificial contraception because God told Adam and Eve to fill the earth. These Christians think that only God can decide who should and should not get pregnant.

However, many Protestant Christians adopt a more flexible approach and will permit the use of artificial contraception – though they still may not use certain types like the morning after pill because fertilisation has already taken place.

Over to you! Give yourself four minutes on the clock and have a go at answering this question. Remember, in order to 'explain' something, you need to **develop** your points. See page 9 for a reminder of how to do this.

WHAT WENT WELL

This student has correctly identified a key Christian belief about contraception, and provided an explanation.

HOW TO IMPROVE

The question asks for two different Christian beliefs, and the beliefs described here reflect one Christian perspective. The student should try to make it as easy as possible for the examiner to award them marks, by giving two different beliefs, both of which are explained. Also, be careful to distinguish between 'natural' and 'artificial' contraception. See the 'improved student response' opposite for suggested corrections.

• Question 'c'

*Question **c** is AO1 – this tests your knowledge and understanding.*

(c) Explain **two** different Christian beliefs about homosexuality. In your answer you must refer to a source of wisdom and authority. (5)

Student response

Many Christians believe that homosexual relationships are wrong: 'Do not have sexual relationships with a man as one does with a woman' (Leviticus 18: 22).

Some more liberal Christians are happy to accept committed homosexual relationships, because they believe that the interpretation of the Bible passages are not clear-cut.

WHAT WENT WELL

This student has correctly identified two Christian beliefs about contraception, and has provided a relevant source of wisdom and authority.

HOW TO IMPROVE

The student should be careful to remember to explain each belief, even when they have included a source of wisdom and authority. The first belief is not explained and needs to be developed. See the 'improved student response' opposite for suggested corrections.

Improved student response

Many Christians believe that homosexual relationships are wrong, because the Bible contains several passages which forbid it: 'Do not have sexual relationships with a man as one does with a woman' (Leviticus 18: 22). They believe it isn't part of God's original plan for creation.

Some more liberal Christians are happy to accept committed homosexual relationships, because they believe that the interpretation of the Bible passages are not clear-cut.

Over to you! Give yourself five minutes on the clock and have a go at answering this question. You need to write two developed points, one of which needs to be supported by a source of wisdom and authority.

• Question 'd'

*Question **d** is AO2 – this tests your ability to evaluate.*

(d) 'Christianity should be more understanding when marriages break down.' Evaluate this statement considering arguments for and against. In your response you should:
- refer to Christian teachings
- refer to different Christian points of view
- refer to non-religious points of view
- reach a justified conclusion. (12)

Student response

Divorce is the legal termination of a marriage, and at certain times in history it has been controversial in society. Within Christianity today, there are different views about divorce.

It could be argued that the Catholic Church would disagree with the claim that Christianity should be more understanding when marriages break down. This is because they don't believe divorce is possible. They believe that marriage is a covenant between both partners and God which cannot be broken. Whilst Catholic Christians would show compassion to those in difficulty, they would nevertheless say that marriage is for life. The Catholic Church does declare a marriage to be null under very specific circumstances, for example if the couple are forced to marry.

Other Christians, for example Anglicans, would say that they do show understanding when marriages break down. They would argue that God forgives mistakes and understands relationship breakdown. Many churches – in all denominations – offer marriage counselling and support to help prevent divorce.

In conclusion, I think that Christianity is, in part, understanding when marriages break down – all Christians would argue that they should show compassion to people in difficulty. However, I think it is better for a marriage to be happy and that they should be allowed to divorce and have the chance at a future with a different partner – and some Christians should be more understanding about that.

WHAT WENT WELL

The student refers to the statement in the question, describes two different Christian points of view, and reaches a justified conclusion.

HOW TO IMPROVE

The student has not referred to non-religious points of view – a requirement of the question. A better answer would also need to include sources of wisdom and authority. Have a look at this improved version of the student response.

Improved student response

Divorce is the legal termination of a marriage, and at certain times in history it has been controversial in society. Within Christianity today, there are different views about divorce.

It could be argued that the Catholic Church would disagree with the claim that Christianity should be more understanding when marriages break down. This is because they don't believe divorce is possible. They believe that marriage is a covenant between both partners and God which cannot be broken: 'what God has joined together, let no one separate'. Whilst Catholic Christians would show compassion to those in difficulty, they would nevertheless say that marriage is for life. The Catholic Church does declare a marriage to be null under very specific circumstances, for example if the couple are forced to marry.

Other Christians, for example Anglicans, would say that they do show understanding when marriages break down. These Christians might argue that Jesus himself mentioned circumstances where divorce is permitted (Matthew 19: 9). They would argue that God forgives mistakes and understands relationship breakdown. Many churches – in all denominations – offer marriage counselling and support to help prevent divorce.

Non-religious people would be more likely to agree that Christians should show more understanding. For example, Humanists do not believe that marriage was established by God. Humanists make decisions based on what would make people happy – and if a marriage is unhappy for those involved, they would support the couple's decision to divorce and remarry someone they are happier with.

In conclusion, I think that Christianity is, in part, understanding when marriages break down – all Christians would argue that they should show compassion to people in difficulty. However, I agree with the non-religious view that it is better for a marriage to be happy and that they should be allowed to divorce and have the chance at a future with a different partner – and some Christians should be more understanding about that.

Over to you! Give yourself 12 minutes on the clock and have a go at answering this question. Remember to refer back to the original statement in your writing when you give different points of view, and make sure you cover each of the bullet points given in the question.

BUILD YOUR SKILLS

In your exams, you'll need to make sure you use religious terminology correctly. Do you know the meaning of the following important terms for this topic?

- sanctity of marriage
- cohabitation
- homosexuality
- nuclear families
- blended families
- rites of passage
- local parish
- family planning
- situation ethics
- prejudice
- discrimination

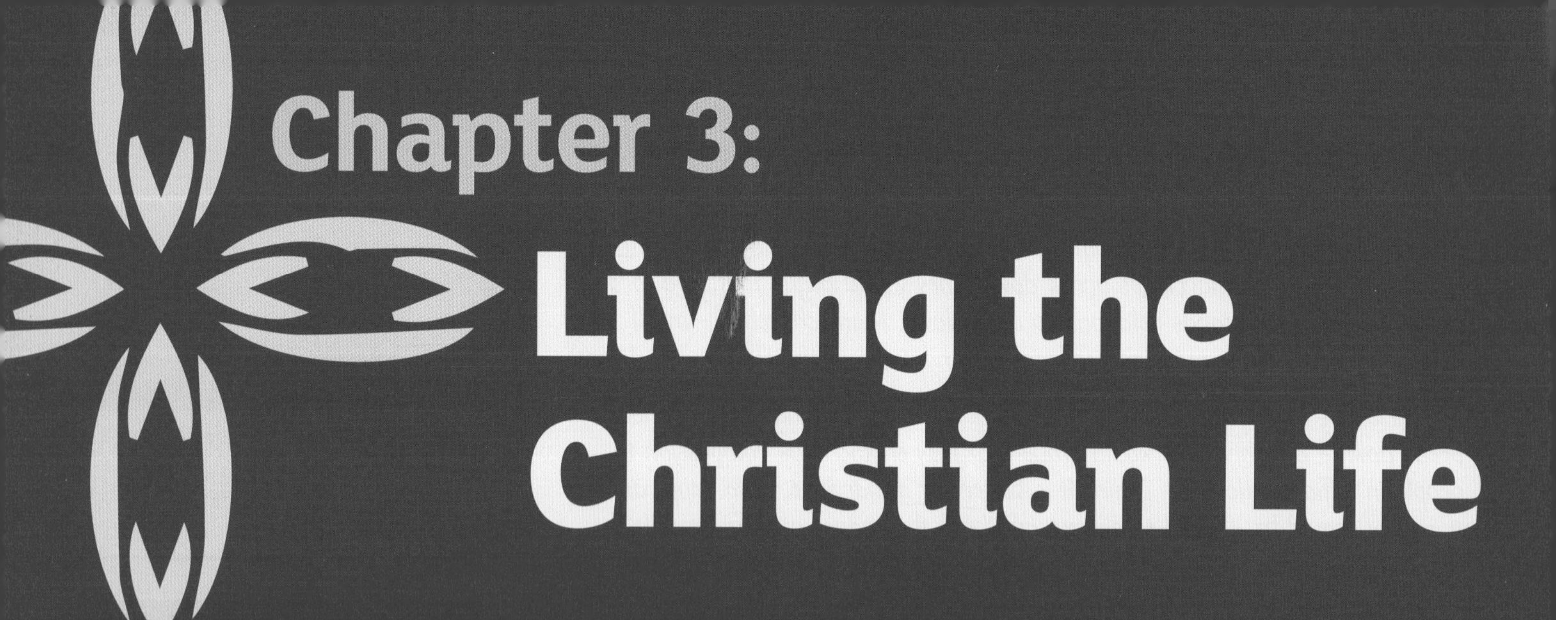

Chapter 3: Living the Christian Life

Christian worship

SPECIFICATION FOCUS

Christian worship: liturgical and non-liturgical forms of worship, including activities which are informal and individual, including reference to the *Book of Common Prayer*; when each form might be used and why; divergent Christian attitudes towards the practices, meaning and significance of liturgical and non-liturgical forms of worship in Christian life today, with reference to denominations which worship with less structure such as some Pentecostal churches.

Living the Christian life is a decision on the part of an individual to live as a follower of Jesus. This chapter looks at the various activities that these followers take part in. Although these activities have strong similarities, there are clearly different emphases and divergent attitudes represented among different Christian **denominations**. These differences are often clearest between one denomination and another, but this is not always the case, and it is worth noting that the larger denominations (for instance Anglicans and Catholics) often have a wide range of styles represented within the same denomination.

Worship is when religious believers express their love and respect for, and devotion to, God. It is a time when Christians can thank God, ask his forgiveness, and pray for themselves, other people and the world at large. It helps them to feel closer to God.

Liturgical and non-liturgical worship

Christians can worship in different ways:

- **liturgical** worship: usually following an agreed form of words (often the congregation follow the words in a service book or on an overhead screen).
- **non-liturgical** worship: although the service will have a clear structure, there will be no, or very few, set words other than the words to songs.
- individual worship: quiet worship alone in a person's own home.

The Anglican Church has both liturgical and non-liturgical services. An Anglican service, from the *Book of Common Prayer* or the more recent service book *Common Worship*, contains set services. The text in ordinary type indicates when the priest or service leader should read, and the text in bold type indicates when everyone should read together. Here is an example from an Anglican communion service:

The Lord be with you
All **and also with you.**

Lift up your hearts.
All **We lift them to the Lord.**

Let us give thanks to the Lord our God.
All **It is right to give thanks and praise.**

It is right to praise you, Father, Lord of all creation;
in your love you made us for yourself.

When we turned away
you did not reject us,
but came to meet us in your Son.
All **You embraced us as your children**
and welcomed us to sit and eat with you.

A The Anglican communion service is an example of liturgical worship

B Various denominations use modern styles of worship in both liturgical and non-liturgical services

> **STRETCH**
> Music is an important feature of liturgical and non-liturgical worship. It is used to praise and express belief in God. Find out what types of music are used in worship and the titles of some specific pieces. Why do you think music like this is so important to worshippers?

Methodists and Catholics have service books like this too. The Anglican denomination also has an informal, non-liturgical service. The structure of that service usually follows a pattern of prayer (see 3.3), sung worship, Bible reading and a **sermon**. There is very little prescription as to what prayers are said or what songs are sung. This style of service might also be found in a Catholic church, but would be more common in Baptist and Pentecostal churches. There would, however, be considerable stylistic differences in the sung worship elements of each of those services. The instruments would also vary from organ music, which might be more familiar in a Methodist or Baptist setting, to brass bands in a Salvation Army setting, to electric guitars and drums in a Pentecostal setting. By this point in the twenty-first-century, however, all styles of instrument and worship could be found in all denominations.

The Book of Common Prayer

The *Book of Common Prayer* (BCP) is the oldest Anglican service book. It was written in the sixteenth century by Thomas Cranmer, and modified in 1662. Many of its prayers and services are still used today. The BCP also contains: the special services for ordaining priests and bishops; baptism, wedding and funeral services; the **creeds**; the 39 Articles (see 3.2); and special prayers for each week of the year. Here is a prayer from the BCP that has been said since the seventeenth century:

> 'Lighten our darkness, we beseech thee, O Lord;
> and by thy great mercy defend us from
> all perils and dangers of this night;
> for the love of thy only Son, our Saviour, Jesus Christ.
> Amen.'
> *From the Book of Common Prayer*

USEFUL TERMS

Creed: a statement of firmly held beliefs; for example, the Apostles' Creed or the Nicene Creed

Denominations: the name given to the main groups within the Church

Liturgical: a set form of worship, usually following agreed words

Non-liturgical: a form of worship which is not set

Sermon: a talk or teaching from a church leader

Worship: believers expressing love and respect for, and devotion to, God

Divergent Christian attitudes

As we have seen, liturgical and non-liturgical forms of worship occur in various different denominations, and most Christians worship using both forms. However, some Christians prefer one over the other. For example, Christians who value liturgical worship find comfort in using words that may well have been said for decades, or, in the case of the *Book of Common Prayer*, for centuries. There is also some security in knowing exactly the pattern the service will follow, the length of time it will take, and usually that the form of words used have been authorised by a particular denominational hierarchy.

The non-liturgical service pattern is far more common in charismatic churches, such as Pentecostal churches and an increasing number of Anglican churches, and in these churches the emphasis is placed on 'following the Spirit'; in other words, listening to God and following his lead in worship. Christians who value non-liturgical worship tend to appreciate the fact that they have more freedom to express their worship – this might involve lifting hands or even dancing. Typically the sung worship element may be of any length, the service may or may not have structured prayers, the service leader has far more control of the service and is able to weave in different aspects, for example a video clip or group discussion. Elements of the service can change during the service, extra songs can be added, or an extended prayer time can be introduced.

Individual worship

Believers often worship God on their own. They may want to praise God for who he is, or so that they can feel closer to him, or they may have a particular problem they want to talk to God about. Individual worship can include prayer, meditation, Bible reading, singing, and quiet thinking.

BUILD YOUR SKILLS

1 Copy and complete the following table for the main ideas about Christian worship in this unit. The first type of worship has been given for you.

Type of worship	What does it involve?	Why is it important for Christians?
Liturgical worship		

2 What is the *Book of Common Prayer* and why is it important to some Christians? Write a short paragraph of explanation.

3 Why might some Christians prefer either liturgical or non-liturgical worship? Try to refer to at least one denomination in your answer.

COMPARE AND CONTRAST

In your exam, you could be asked to **compare and contrast** Christian worship with the practices of another religion you are studying. Create a table that explains the similarities and differences among them.

SUMMARY

- Worship is important because it helps believers express love for God.
- It can be liturgical, non-liturgical, or individual.
- There is a great amount of variety in worship both among and within denominations.

EXAM-STYLE QUESTIONS

a Outline **three** ways a Christian can worship. (3)

b Describe **two** differences between Christian worship and that of another religion you have studied. (4)

3.2 The sacraments

What are sacraments?

The **sacraments** are particularly important and significant Christian ceremonies. Many Christians think of the sacraments as signs of God's love – a special holy action that shows a religious truth. For some Christians, for example Catholics, sacraments are more than just signs – they are 'effective signs', which means that they bring about the thing that they symbolise. For instance, **baptism** is not just a sign of the forgiveness of sins, it actually brings about the forgiveness of sins.

For something to be a sacrament, it has to be officially recognised by the Church as having been established by Jesus. Churches differ on this matter. Therefore, some ceremonies, such as marriage, might be carried out in all churches, but might not be considered to be an official sacrament in all churches.

The sacraments recognised by different groups

Various denominations within the Church have different views on the sacraments. The biggest denominations are the Catholic, Orthodox and Protestant Churches. In turn, Protestants are divided into groups, such as Anglicans (including the Church of England) and Non-Conformists (e.g. Quakers, Methodists, Salvation Army, and Baptists).

The Catholic Council of Trent (1545–1563) agreed that there were seven sacraments (see image **A**). The Orthodox Church also recognises seven sacraments. In contrast, the Church of England met in 1562 to agree the **39 Articles of Religion**, and Article 25 stated that the Church of England would only recognise two sacraments – baptism and the **Eucharist**. In some Protestant churches, for example the Salvation Army and Quakers, no sacraments are officially recognised.

SPECIFICATION FOCUS

The role of the sacraments in Christian life and their practice in two denominations: the role of the sacraments/ordinance as a whole; the nature and importance of the meaning and celebration of baptism and the Eucharist in at least two denominations including reference to the 39 Articles XXV–XXXVI; divergent Christian attitudes towards the use and number of sacraments in Orthodox, Catholic and Protestant traditions.

USEFUL TERMS

39 Articles of Religion: a historical record of beliefs (or 'doctrines') held by the Church of England

Anoint: apply oil to a person's head as a sign of holiness and God's approval

Sacrament: an important Christian ceremony

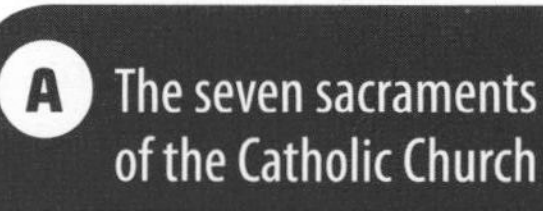

A The seven sacraments of the Catholic Church

Sacraments of initiation			Sacraments of service		Sacraments of healing	
Baptism	Confirmation	Eucharist (mass or holy communion)	Marriage	Taking holy orders	Reconciliation (confession)	**Anointing** the sick with oil

The 39 Articles of Religion

In the mid-sixteenth century, the Church of England had recently split from the Catholic Church, and was feeling the influence of various Protestant denominations. Therefore, in 1562, the bishops and archbishops of England came together to discuss matters of belief. Their eventual agreed beliefs would be published under the heading of the 39 Articles. The Articles cover heaven, hell, baptism, creeds, and much more, but the Articles also make some strong statements against various areas of Catholic belief. From that point onwards, priests of the Church of England would need to agree to the 39 Articles before they could be ordained.

> **There are two Sacraments ordained of Christ our Lord in the Gospel, that is to say, Baptism, and the Supper of the Lord.** Those five commonly called Sacraments, that is to say, Confirmation, Penance, Orders, Matrimony, and extreme Unction, are not to be counted for Sacraments of the Gospel...
> *(From Article XXV of the 39 Articles of Religion)*

Celebrating the sacraments

The sacraments have two important aspects:

- **Physical side:** this can be felt, touched, seen, smelled or tasted, as, for example, the bread and wine in the Eucharist.
- **Spiritual side:** each sacrament brings a spiritual blessing to the person involved.

Each sacrament has its own special ceremony, which includes some or all of the following features: saying prayers, singing hymns, making vows, or promises, listening to Bible readings, listening to a sermon.

USEFUL TERMS

Baptism: the Christian ceremony that welcomes a person into the Christian community

Eucharist: the ceremony commemorating the Last Supper, involving bread and wine; also called Holy Communion or Mass

Baptism

Baptism is the ceremony in which a person formally becomes a member of the Church. It was commanded by Jesus in *Matthew 28: 19*.

> Therefore go and make disciples of all nations, **baptising them** in the name of the Father and of the Son and of the Holy Spirit...
> *(Matthew 28: 19)*

The Catholic, Orthodox and Anglican Churches all celebrate baptism of infants (babies and young children). The Quakers and Salvation Army do not have formal baptism at all. The Baptist Church baptises people it considers old enough to decide for themselves that they want to be baptised.

In an infant baptism, a priest pours water three times on the child's head to show that the Trinity has come into their life and that their sins have been washed away. The child's parents and godparents publicly declare their beliefs, and hold a lighted candle to symbolise that they and the child have passed from the darkness of sin into the light of Jesus. In the Catholic Church, the candle is lit from the Paschal candle as a sign of faith in the resurrection of Jesus. The child is then welcomed as a member of the Church.

What symbolism can you see in this photo? Can you find out its significance?

B An infant being baptised into the Catholic Church

Some denominations, for example Baptist and Pentecostal Churches, do not celebrate infant baptism, and instead baptise people when they are adults. This is because they believe baptism is a choice that should be made as an adult. They do celebrate the birth of infants, however, and usually have a 'dedication' service in which the parents and the church community promise to bring up the child according to Christian values.

Confirmation

When a person freely chooses to conclude the process of baptism, as already begun during their baptism as an infant, they are 'confirmed', usually after attending a course of Bible study. Anglicans usually have to be at least

12 years old to be confirmed, Catholics have to be at least 8 years old. There is no confirmation service in the Orthodox Church, and instead of confirmation, Orthodox Christians have the sacrament of Chrismation, which immediately follows baptism, and involves being anointed with holy oil called Chrism.

The confirmation service is held by the local bishop. Those being confirmed make the same statements of belief as the parents in an infant baptism. The bishop lays hands on the person's head as a sign that the Holy Spirit has entered into the person's life. (In the Catholic Church, the laying on of hands is what actually brings about the gift of the Spirit). The person is then welcomed as a full member of the Church.

Eucharist

The Eucharist is accepted by most Christians as a re-enactment of the final meal that Jesus shared with his disciples. At that meal, he spoke of bread and wine as being his body and blood.

The Eucharist is called Mass in the Catholic Church, Holy Communion in the Anglican Church and the Lord's Supper by the Methodists. It is not celebrated by the Salvation Army.

In Catholic and Anglican churches today, the priest prays for God's special blessing on bread and wine, which makes them holy. They are then given by the priest to each person taking part in the Eucharist. Only those who are baptised or confirmed may take part. They each take a small piece of bread or a wafer and a sip from a single cup (chalice) of wine. In the Orthodox Church, Christians receive bread soaked in wine.

Not all Christians see the Eucharist in the same way:

- Catholic and Orthodox Christians believe that the bread and wine change to become the actual body and blood of Jesus. In the Catholic Church this change happens when the bread and wine are blessed and is called transubstantiation. In the Orthodox Church, how or when the bread and wine change is believed to be a mystery.
- Other Christians, including Anglicans, believe that the bread and wine are simply symbolic of Jesus' body and blood to help believers remember his death.
- Catholics believe they should receive the bread and wine at least once a week and some receive it every day.
- Protestants may take the bread and wine less often, perhaps once every few weeks. Some do not receive it at all, for example members of the Salvation Army.

Marriage

The sacrament of marriage reflects God's everlasting love. It is the legal union of a man and a woman, who promise before God that they will love, honour, cherish, and respect each other through sickness, health, through good times and bad times, until they are parted by death.

Taking holy orders

In the Catholic and Orthodox Churches, the sacrament of holy orders means becoming a deacon, priest, or bishop.

> 'And he took bread, gave thanks and broke it, and gave it to them, saying, "This is my body given for you; do this in remembrance of me." In the same way, after the supper he took the cup, saying, "This cup is the new covenant in my blood, which is poured out for you.'
> *(Luke 22: 19–20)*

SUPPORT

The **covenant** is an agreement between God and humans, which says that because Jesus died to save people from sin, those who believe in him will have everlasting life in heaven with God.

C The Eucharist involves bread and wine

Catholics believe that priests are descended from Jesus' original Apostles 2,000 years ago. As a result, priests receive the grace and power of the Holy Spirit and have the privileged ability to administer all of the sacraments apart from the sacrament of holy orders. Deacons can administer the sacraments of baptism and marriage, and both priests and deacons can preach.

Like Catholic priests, bishops in the Orthodox Church are believed to be the direct successors of the original Apostles. Orthodox bishops are required to remain celibate, but priests may be married before they are ordained.

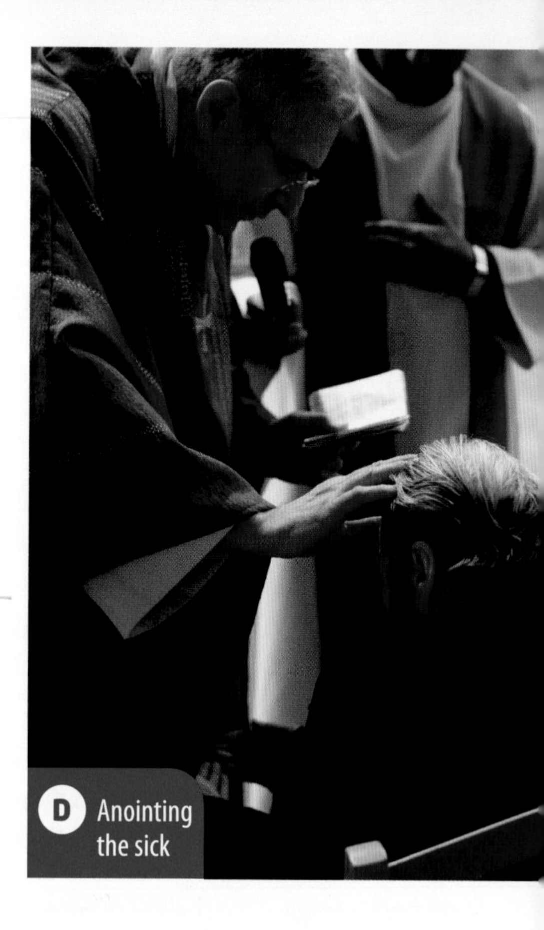
D Anointing the sick

Reconciliation

The sacrament of reconciliation (also called confession) is when a person asks forgiveness for the wrongs they have done. For reconciliation to be effective, the person must be genuinely sorry, have spent time preparing their confession, and be ready to receive God's blessing and forgiveness. In return, they know they have done what they could to right the wrong.

Catholic and Orthodox Christians confess their sins to a priest, who, as God's representative on earth, will then give them God's forgiveness. This may involve the person having to 'do penance', such as saying a particular prayer a set number of times, or carrying out positive actions to right the wrongs caused by their sins.

Anointing the sick

The sacrament of anointing the sick is based on teaching in the Bible:

> 'Is anyone among you ill? Let them call the elders of the church to pray over them and anoint them with oil in the name of the Lord.'
> *(James 5: 14)*

In the anointing ceremony, the sick person confesses their sins and prays with the priest. They pray that God will heal them or, if they are dying, that God will forgive their sins and grant them everlasting life in heaven. The priest lays hands on the person to enable God's love to work within them and some olive oil is gently rubbed onto their forehead.

BUILD YOUR SKILLS

1 Copy and complete the following table for the main ideas about the sacraments in this unit.

Sacrament	What is involved?	Which Christians recognise it and why?

2 Explain two different approaches to baptism within Christianity.

3 Can the bread and wine really be the body and blood of Jesus? Explain your ideas, referring to different Christian views.

? EXAM-STYLE QUESTIONS

a Outline **three** Christian sacraments. (3)

b Explain **two** reasons why sacraments are important to Christians. (4)

SUMMARY

- The sacraments are significant Christian ceremonies which have been recognised by the Church.
- The Catholic and Orthodox Churches recognise seven sacraments, the Church of England recognise two (baptism and the Eucharist), and some churches do not officially recognise any.

3.3 Prayer

SPECIFICATION FOCUS

The nature and purpose of prayer: the nature of and examples of the different types of prayer; set prayers; informal prayer and the Lord's Prayer including Matthew 6: 5–14; when each type might be used and why; divergent Christian attitudes towards the importance of each type of prayer for Christians today.

What is prayer?

Prayer is a way of communicating with God, usually through words, and having a personal relationship with him. Prayer may offer praise or thanks to God or ask him for forgiveness or other specific things, for example good health. Christians can pray in many different ways – using set or informal prayers, in public or in private, every day or on special occasions.

Set prayers

Most prayers in an Anglican or Catholic church service are set and formal. They are usually read or sung from a text, such as the *Book of Common Prayer*, and follow a set pattern very familiar to believers. The most famous formal prayer is the Lord's Prayer (see figure **A**), which Jesus taught to his followers. It is a special prayer because it covers the needs of all believers.

USEFUL TERMS

Prayer: a way of communicating with God

Informal prayer

Some prayer is much more informal. This type of prayer features in evangelical and charismatic churches, where prayers are not often written down. Instead, prayer tends to be much more spontaneous, because believers say that they are led by the Holy Spirit to choose words to express how they feel at the time.

A What does the Lord's Prayer mean?

'Our Father in heaven,	This is a personal and loving response to God.
hallowed be your name,	Your name is holy and special.
your kingdom come,	May God's kingdom come to our world.
your will be done,	May God's will be carried out.
on earth as it is in heaven.	May God be in charge.
Give us today our daily bread.	Give us all we need to survive.
And forgive us our debts,	Forgive the wrongs we have done.
as we also have forgiven our debtors.	Help us to forgive those who have wronged us.
And lead us not into temptation,	Keep us from being tempted to do wrong.
but deliver us from the evil one.'	Keep us from doing evil.

(Matthew 6: 9–13)

B Many Christians feel better by being able to talk directly and privately to God

Private prayer

Believers can also pray in private settings, such as their own homes. They might say their prayers aloud or offer them silently to God.

> ‘When you pray, go into your room, close the door and pray to your father, who is unseen. Then your Father, who sees what is done in secret, will reward you.’
> *(Matthew 6: 6)*

Special purposes of prayer

Christians use different prayers, depending on what they want to say to God. These can be grouped into different types:

Thanksgiving: to thank God for all that they have.
Contrition: to tell God what they have done wrong and ask for forgiveness.
Supplication: to ask God for something for themselves or others.
Intercession: to ask God to help other people.
Worship: to give honour and respect to God.

Divergent Christian attitudes

Most Christians will use both set and informal prayer to communicate with God. The Lord's Prayer is used regularly in most denominations, as Christians like to follow the example set by Jesus. Christians who prefer to pray using set prayers find comfort in using words that have been said throughout history and that have been authorised by their Church. Reciting these aloud as a community also increases a sense of shared belief and unity. Christians who prefer praying informally might particularly appreciate the personal nature of communicating how they are feeling with God. These Christians also value praying aloud in groups, and those with them will often say 'Amen' after an individual has prayed to show that they agree with the prayer.

C *Praying hands*, a drawing by Albrecht Dürer (c. 1508CE)

BUILD YOUR SKILLS

1. Read the Lord's Prayer on page 87. What different things do Christians ask for or say in this prayer? SUPPORT
2. Why do Christians pray? Write a short paragraph to explain.
3. If God knows everything, what is the point of praying? What would a Christian argue? STRETCH

SUMMARY

- Prayers can be set, informal or private.
- There are prayers for different purposes, and believers differ in their views on the importance of certain types of prayer.

EXAM-STYLE QUESTIONS

b. Explain **two** reasons why prayer is important to Christians. (4)
d. 'Prayer should be informal.' Evaluate this statement considering arguments for and against. In your response you should:
   - refer to Christian teachings
   - refer to different Christian points of view
   - reach a justified conclusion. (15)

3.4 Pilgrimage

SPECIFICATION FOCUS

Pilgrimage: the nature, history and purpose of pilgrimage, including interpretations of Luke 2: 41–43; the significance of the places people go on pilgrimage; divergent Christian teachings about whether pilgrimage is important for Christians today, with specific reference to Catholic and Protestant understandings; the activities associated with, and significance of, Jerusalem, Iona, Taizé and Walsingham.

What is pilgrimage?

A **pilgrimage** is a special journey to a place of religious significance. It is undertaken by a pilgrim, who is making the journey in order to increase their religious faith. It may be a long journey to another country or a shorter one to a sacred place nearer to home.

The first Christian pilgrimages date from the fourth century, when travellers visited the Holy Land (now called Israel) to see places linked to the life of Jesus. Early pilgrims also visited Rome, other sites linked to the Apostles and the saints, and places where **visions** of the Virgin Mary were said to have occurred.

Today, pilgrimage is still popular, with Christians making journeys to Rome, the Holy Land, and **shrines** all around the world. A pilgrimage should have a real impact on the pilgrim and involve some or all of the following aspects: feeling closer to God, discovering special rituals, objects and places, having religious and spiritual experiences, praying and meditating, seeking a cure for sickness.

SUPPORT

What do you think believers gain from pilgrimage? Is it just a religious holiday?

STRETCH

The Canterbury Tales, written by Geoffrey Chaucer around 1390 CE, is a collection of stories told by pilgrims on a pilgrimage from London to Canterbury Cathedral.

Divergent Christian views on pilgrimage

The Catholic Church teaches about the importance of pilgrimage in the Christian life:

> 'Pilgrimages evoke our earthly journey toward heaven and are traditionally very special occasions for renewal in prayer.'
> *Catechism of the Catholic Church, 2691*

In other words, pilgrimages are believed to be a special opportunity to pray and experience closeness to God. In many Protestant Churches, pilgrimage is equally important, although the sites of significance may sometimes be different (for example, Christians who do not recognise the authority of the Pope, as Catholics do, may not view a pilgrimage to Rome in the same way).

Some Protestant Churches do not place as much emphasis on pilgrimage. Whilst journeying and praying for the sake of God is something they might encourage, pilgrimage is not considered by them to be a central part of Christian life.

A A medieval pilgrimage

The pilgrimage to Jerusalem

The most famous place of Christian pilgrimage is Jerusalem in Israel (the Holy Land). It is where most of Jesus' ministry took place, so pilgrims feel it is important to go to different sites in the city to think about the events that took place there.

In the Gospel of Luke, Jesus himself made a pilgrimage with his parents to Jerusalem, at the age of 12. When it was time to leave, his parents could not find Jesus. When they finally found him, he was in the temple, sitting and listening to teachers, and he said: 'Why were you searching for me? […] Didn't you know I had to be in my Father's house?' (*Luke 2: 49*). Modern pilgrims aim to follow Jesus' example and look for opportunities to be close to God. Pilgrims today visit:

- The Mount of Olives, where Jesus often taught his followers
- The room of the Last Supper
- The Garden of Gethsemane, where Jesus was arrested
- The Western Wall, remains of the Temple
- The tomb of the Virgin Mary
- The Church of the Holy Sepulchre, where Jesus was crucified and buried

B Modern pilgrims on the Via Dolorosa, the road believed to have been taken by Jesus on his way to be crucified

The pilgrimage to Iona

Iona Abbey, on the island of Iona, off the west coast of Scotland, is one of the UK's oldest sites of pilgrimage. It was founded by St Columba in 563 CE and became the focal point for the spread of Christianity throughout Scotland. The abbey was extensively restored in 1899 and in 1938, when the Iona Community was founded. This Christian community is based on worship, peace and social justice, and welcomes all believers to share in this ministry today.

The pilgrimage to Taizé

Another important place for Christian pilgrimage today is a monastic order in the small village of Taizé in central France. The Taizé Community was founded by Roger Schütz, known as Brother Roger, in 1940. Today, it has over 100 members, and thousands of pilgrims visit to share the community's way of life.

The community prays together three times a day and is devoted to peace and justice through prayer and meditation. It seeks to unite people of all races and encourages pilgrims to live in the spirit of kindness, simplicity, and reconciliation. Importance is also placed on music, including songs and chants in many languages.

SUPPORT

People who live **monastic** lives, such as **monks** and **nuns**, have chosen to dedicate their lives to prayer and worship, usually whilst living in a **monastery** with others.

The pilgrimage to Walsingham

A popular English site for Christian pilgrimage is the Shrine of Our Lady of Walsingham in Norfolk.

It is said to be the place where Lady Richeldis de Faverches saw a vision of the Virgin Mary in 1061CE. According to tradition, the Virgin showed Lady Richeldis a vision of the house where the Angel Gabriel told Mary that she would be the mother of Jesus. Lady Richeldis built a copy of the house on the spot where she had the vision. Known as the Holy House, it became a place of pilgrimage.

In the centuries that followed, thousands of pilgrims went to Walsingham, including Henry VIII and Queen Catherine of Aragon. Later in Henry's reign, the shrine was destroyed.

After restoration, Walsingham was re-opened to regular pilgrimage in the 1920s. In 1938 it was enlarged to form the area known today, including a Catholic shrine, an Anglican shrine and the Orthodox Church of St Seraphim. There are often, therefore, pilgrimages of mixed denominations to Walsingham.

USEFUL TERMS

Pilgrimage: a journey to a religious or holy place

Shrine: a holy place

Vision: seeing or hearing someone or something holy

BUILD YOUR SKILLS

1 Copy and complete the following table for important pilgrimage sites.

Site of pilgrimage	What does it represent?	Why is it important for Christians?
Jerusalem		
Iona		
Taizé		
Walsingham		

2 a Which of the following statements, if any, do you agree with? Explain why.
- 'Some sites of pilgrimage are more convincing than others.'
- 'Pilgrims are just wishful thinkers.'
- 'Pilgrimage is still important in today's world.'
- 'On pilgrimage, the journey is as important as the destination.'

b With a partner, discuss whether pilgrimages are worthwhile or a waste of time.

3 Many thousands of young people visit Taizé each year (see image **C**). Do you think they have to be Christians to benefit from the visit? Why/why not?

C Worship at Taizé

SUMMARY

- Pilgrimage has a very long history and is still important today.
- Jerusalem, Iona, Taizé and Walsingham are important pilgrimage sites.
- Pilgrimage helps believers to understand more about God and their faith.
- It can give believers a strong religious or spiritual experience.

EXAM-STYLE QUESTIONS

a Outline **three** reasons why pilgrimage is important to Christians. (3)

d 'Every Christian should go on a pilgrimage.'
Evaluate this statement considering arguments for and against. In your response you should:
- refer to Christian teachings
- refer to different Christian points of view
- reach a justified conclusion.

(15)

3.5 Christian celebrations

SPECIFICATION FOCUS

Christian religious celebrations: the nature and history of Christian festivals in the church year, including Christmas and Easter; the significance of celebrating Advent and Christmas; the significance of celebrating Holy Week and Easter, with reference to interpretations of 1 Corinthians 15: 12–34.

Christians use celebrations to remember and give thanks for the most important events in their faith. Celebrations take different forms to reflect the nature of the event. Some, like Christmas and Easter Sunday, are times of great rejoicing. Others, such as Good Friday, are times for quiet reflection.

Christmas

There are two accounts of the birth of Jesus, given in the Gospels of Luke and Matthew. According to Luke's Gospel, God sent the Angel Gabriel to tell a woman called Mary, who was a virgin, that she would be the mother of God's son. She accepted God's will and became pregnant. She and her husband Joseph travelled to the town of Bethlehem. There, she gave birth to Jesus and was visited by shepherds. The Gospel of Matthew includes an account of the visit of the wise men, or 'Magi', from the east.

The whole season of Christmastide runs for 12 nights after 25 December to 6 January, which is when Jesus was shown to the wise men. The 6 January is therefore called **Epiphany** or Twelfth Night.

As a festival, Christmas shares much in common with other festivals at that time.

- It is just after mid-winter, when the sun begins to shine more and the days start to grow longer.
- It is near the Winter Solstice, when mistletoe was seen as a sign of God's blessing.
- Holly, also a Christian symbol, was used by ancient people as a protection from evil.

In medieval times, Christmas was a time for feasting and fun. However, in the seventeenth century, people were not allowed to have celebrations because they were believed by Puritans to be excessive and a distraction from core Christian beliefs. In 1644 Christmas was banned altogether. Christmas became popular again in the nineteenth century when cards, decorations and Christmas trees were introduced.

Today, Christian churches hold special services, including carol services and a **vigil** before Christmas, midnight mass on Christmas Eve, and a special service of celebration on Christmas morning, which may include a **nativity** play.

USEFUL TERMS

Advent: a season of preparation for Christmas

Epiphany: a moment of suddenly revealing something surprising or great

Holy Week: the week before Easter

Nativity: the birth of someone

Prophecy: a message from God in which he communicates his will

Vigil: staying awake at night in order to pray; also the name given to the celebration of a festival on the eve before the festival itself

A Children's nativity plays are an important part of church life

B Candlelight vigil

Advent

Advent starts on the Sunday nearest 30 November. It marks the start of the Christian year and is a time of preparation for Christmas. On the first Sunday of Advent, Christians light one of the four candles on Advent wreaths. On each of the next three Sundays before Christmas, they light one more candle. This is to remember the 'light' of Jesus that is about to come into the world.

Holy Week

Holy Week is the week just before Easter, beginning with Palm Sunday and ending with Holy Saturday. It is the final week of Lent, the six-week period of self-examination when most Christians pray, say sorry and try to make amends for their wrongdoings, fast, and give to the poor in preparation for celebrating Jesus' resurrection on Easter Sunday. Holy Week is also a time of solemn church services, as Christians remember the final days and death of Jesus. The following events are remembered during the week:

- **Palm Sunday:** Jesus' arrival in Jerusalem on a donkey, when huge crowds greeted him and threw down palm leaves. This fulfilled an ancient **prophecy** that the Messiah would arrive in this way. Today, Christians receive small palm crosses to remind them of the prophecy and the death of Jesus.
- **Holy Monday:** Mary anointing Jesus with oil at Bethany as a sign of God's approval *(John 12:3)*.
- **Holy Tuesday:** Jesus predicting that Judas would betray him and Peter would deny that he knew Jesus.
- **Holy Wednesday:** Judas arranging with the high priests to betray Jesus.
- **Maundy Thursday:** Jesus washing the disciples' feet and the Last Supper. The washing of feet was a symbolic act to show that the disciples must be humble and serve others ('Maundy' means 'commandment'). On this day, churches may hold a meal reflecting the original Last Supper.
- **Good Friday:** Jesus' death on the cross. For Christians, this is a solemn day of processions or re-enacting the events leading up to the crucifixion.
- **Holy Saturday:** Jesus going to hell and preaching to the dead. In the evening, many Christians hold a vigil. For example, on the eve of Holy Saturday, Catholic Christians have an Easter vigil at which they celebrate the resurrection of Jesus. This is the most solemn liturgy that the Catholic Church celebrates.

'Shout, daughter of Jerusalem! See your king comes to you, righteous and having salvation, gentle and riding on a donkey.' *(Zechariah 9: 9)*

'I tell you the truth, one of you is going to betray me.' *(John 13: 20)*

'A new command I give you: Love one another.' *(John 13: 34)*

Easter Sunday

Easter Sunday celebrates the resurrection of Jesus from the dead. Jesus had been buried in a cave tomb with an enormous stone rolled across the entrance. On Sunday morning, Mary Magdalene, then others of Jesus' followers, found that the stone had been rolled away and the tomb was empty. Soon after, they saw Jesus – he had risen from the dead.

In *1 Corinthians 15*, Paul writes to the Corinthian church about the resurrection. Members of the church at the time were in disagreement about whether the dead could be raised. Paul emphasises the fundamental importance of the resurrection to Christianity:

> ‘For what I received I passed on to you as of first importance: that Christ died for our sins according to the Scriptures, that he was buried, that he was raised on the third day...’
> *(1 Corinthians 15: 3–4)*

He writes, 'by this gospel you are saved' (*1 Corinthians 15: 2*), in other words Christians have access to eternal life because of the resurrection of Jesus.

> ‘And if Christ has not been raised, our preaching is useless and so is your faith.’
> *(1 Corinthians 15: 14)*

Most Christians today believe in the physical resurrection of Jesus, but some more liberal Christians believe that the resurrection should be interpreted metaphorically. Mainstream and liberal Christians alike celebrate this story on Easter Sunday, worshipping and praising Jesus in church services.

C The empty tomb; which people can you see represented here?

STRETCH

Read the rest of Paul's argument in *1 Corinthians 15: 12–34*. What are his key points?

BUILD YOUR SKILLS

1. Explain the significance of each of the following: Christmas, Advent, Holy Week, Easter.
2. Which of the following statements, if any, do you agree with? Explain why.
   - 'Easter is about the death of Jesus, not about Easter eggs.'
   - 'The most important Christian celebration day is Easter Sunday.'
   - 'Religious celebrations have no importance in today's world.'
3. According to Paul, why is the resurrection of Jesus so important?

SUMMARY

- Christian celebrations include Advent, Christmas, Holy Week, and Easter.
- These celebrations help believers to remember the importance of events in Jesus' life.
- They also help believers to feel closer to God and understand more about their faith.

EXAM-STYLE QUESTIONS

a Outline **three** features of Christmas for Christians. (3)

d 'Easter is the most important Christian festival.'
Evaluate this statement considering arguments for and against. In your response you should:
- refer to Christian teachings
- refer to different Christian points of view
- reach a justified conclusion. (15)

3.6 The future of the Church

Growth of the Christian Church

Christianity has more followers than any other religion and **Pentecostalism** is one of the fastest growing denominations. There are 2.4 billion Christians in the world today and the number is growing. The biggest increases recently have been in Africa, where there are 541 million Christians, with 33,000 people joining the faith every day. The Church is also growing in Asia and the Middle East, especially in Nepal, China, and Saudi Arabia.

Much of this growth is due to the work of **missionaries**, who preach from the Bible and invite people to **convert** to the Christian faith. However, people in many countries are also actively turning away from traditional beliefs to join faiths that seem to offer more – enthusiasm, lively worship, and a promise of eternal life.

Christianity in the UK

In contrast, the Christian Church in the UK and Western Europe is going through a difficult time. A recent survey noted that although 64 per cent of UK residents say they are Christian, the number of local churchgoers is falling quite rapidly. Many churches closed between 2010 and 2016 – 168 Anglican, 500 Methodist and 100 Catholic.

However, the numbers of people joining Pentecostal and evangelical churches has been steadily increasing. Between 2010 and 2016, 600 Pentecostal churches opened. This growth seems to be driven in part by people coming to live in the UK, particularly from Africa, the Caribbean and South America, but these churches have also seen a steady increase in UK worshippers.

Christian missionary work

The Church has a **mission** to spread the Christian faith. It does this by sending missionaries around the world. As well as preaching to people about Jesus, missionary work may also include working among the poor to build hospitals and schools, nursing, and teaching.

SPECIFICATION FOCUS

The future of the Christian Church: Church growth, the history and purpose of missionary and evangelical work including reference to Mark 16: 9–20 and John 20: 21–22; divergent ways this is put into practice by Church locally, nationally and globally; Christian attitudes to why evangelical work is important for the Church and for individual Christians.

USEFUL TERMS

Convert: to change from one set of beliefs to another

Mission: sending individuals or groups to spread the Christian message

Missionary: a person who preaches and invites people to convert to the Christian faith

Pentecostalism: a Protestant movement that puts special emphasis on a direct and personal relationship with God through the Holy Spirit

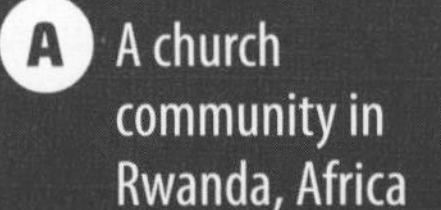

A A church community in Rwanda, Africa

The history of missionary work

The first missionaries were the original followers of Jesus, who obeyed his command called the Great Commission. With the help of the Holy Spirit, the followers were commanded to preach the gospel to all of creation:

> He said to them, "**Go into all the world and preach the gospel to all creation**. Whoever believes and is baptized will be saved, but whoever does not believe will be condemned."
> *(Mark 16: 15)*

> Again Jesus said, "Peace be with you! As the Father has sent me, I am sending you." And with that he breathed on them and said, "**Receive the Holy Spirit...**"
> *(John 20: 21–22)*

The most famous early missionary was St Paul, whose mission took him as far as Rome – thousands of miles from where he began. In the following centuries, Christian missionaries went to many other parts of the world.

Purposes of missionary work

- Inviting non-Christians to convert to Christianity
- Spreading the teachings of Jesus
- Establishing monasteries and churches
- Setting up and running schools and colleges
- Translating the Bible into every language
- Providing sanitation and clean water
- Setting up and staffing hospitals and medical centres

Missionary work today

Many Christians still feel the responsibility to tell others of their faith. Whilst some become missionaries, others show their faith at home in the way they conduct their everyday lives.

Most Christian countries still send missionaries abroad, but they also receive them from elsewhere. Typically, the UK sends out 15,000 missionaries a year, whilst 10,000 others travel into the UK.

However, some people criticise missionary work abroad on the basis that missionaries:

- might only spread Western values
- can infect local populations with foreign germs and diseases
- have caused conflicts and even wars in the past
- could be accused of using natural disasters as an opportunity to 'convert' those who are suffering.

B A school in Cambodia set up by missionaries

The growth of the Pentecostal Church in Britain is also a type of 'reverse mission', with immigrants drawing people back into churches here.

On a local level, churches are encouraged to be open and welcoming to everyone, not just practising Christians, often holding events to draw non-believers in.

Christian evangelistic work

Missionary work involves **evangelism**, preaching the Christian faith in order to invite those of other faiths or none to convert to Christianity. Evangelists are often missionaries, but they might be skilled in preaching to large numbers in their own country.

Evangelists are inspired by biblical teaching to speak clearly, fearlessly and respectfully, and see themselves as following a call from God.

> 'Pray also for me [...] so that I will fearlessly make known the mystery of the gospel...'
> *(Ephesians 6: 19)*

SUPPORT The word **evangelism** comes from the Greek word euaggellion, which means gospel or good news.

Purposes of evangelism
- Preaching the gospel
- Explaining the teachings of Jesus
- Calling people to follow Jesus
- Persuading people to turn to God and reject evil
- Warning people about the consequences of sin

USEFUL TERMS

Alpha: a course run by churches and local Christian groups which enables people to find out more about the Christian faith in a relaxed setting

Evangelism: preaching the gospel in order to attract new believers

Evangelism today

Modern evangelists can be very public figures. Some use television, radio, the Internet, social media, drama, music or comedy to communicate their message. A few appear on television's 'God Channel'. Others speak to huge crowds at Christian events.

However, for many Christians today, evangelism is something that happens naturally in conversation and discussion, as they talk about their faith with others.

CASE STUDY: ALPHA

One organised way that churches enable evangelism in a relaxed format is through **Alpha**, which was started in an Anglican church in 1977. At first, it aimed to help church members understand the basics of the Christian faith. It soon began to be used as an introduction for anyone interested in learning about Christianity.

It now offers 'an opportunity to explore the meaning of life' through a series of talks and discussions in all sorts of places from homes to offices, churches to prisons. The idea has now been adopted by other denominations worldwide and has generated related courses such as relationship courses.

C A group of young people taking part in Alpha

STRETCH Find out more about Alpha by visiting **uk.alpha.org**. What happens on a typical course? What questions do people discuss?

The importance of evangelistic work

This work is important for the Church as a whole and for individual Christians. It:

- enables Christians to obey the Great Commission of Jesus
- encourages Christians to tell other people about their faith
- can help the poor and suffering to have hope
- can occur alongside improvements to education and healthcare
- keeps the Christian message alive and relevant to life today
- brings many new Christians to the Church.

BUILD YOUR SKILLS

1 Copy and complete the following table for Christian missionary and evangelical work.

	What does it mean?	Examples	Why is it important for Christians?
Christian mission			
Evangelism			

2 a Imagine a conversation about evangelism between three teenagers – one is an evangelical Christian, one is a member of another faith, and the third is an atheist. Write a short conversation between them in which:
- each says why their view is right
- each tries to prove that the others are wrong.

b Which teenager do you think offers the best answers? Why?

3 a With a partner or in a group, discuss the advantages and disadvantages of:
- evangelising on television
- taking part in the Alpha Course.

b Write down your conclusions.

SUMMARY

- Christian Church membership is growing globally, but is falling in the UK.
- Missionary and evangelical work preach the Christian faith and invite people to convert to Christianity.
- Missionaries also help the needy.

EXAM-STYLE QUESTIONS

a Outline **three** purposes of Christian missionary work. (3)

c Explain **two** reasons why evangelism is important to Christians. In your answer you must refer to a source of wisdom and authority. (5)

3.7 The local church

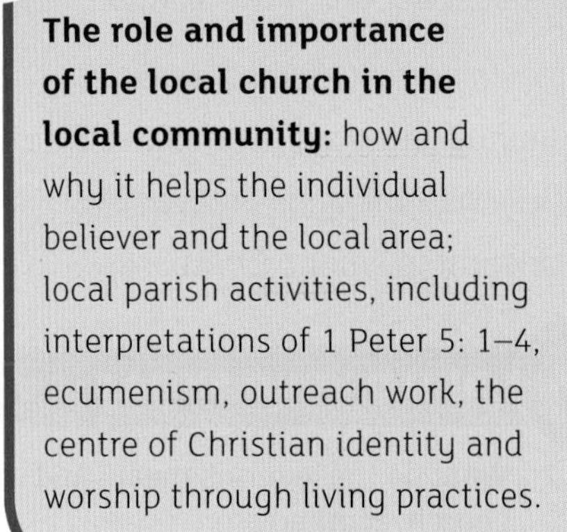

SPECIFICATION FOCUS

The role and importance of the local church in the local community: how and why it helps the individual believer and the local area; local parish activities, including interpretations of 1 Peter 5: 1–4, ecumenism, outreach work, the centre of Christian identity and worship through living practices.

The importance of the local church to the parish

Most Christians belong to a **parish** – a community of local believers within a particular denomination. The care of the parish and its people is entrusted to a parish priest. The local church building plays an important role in the community's life together. Living in that community encourages individual Christians to put their faith into action in everyday living practices, such as being a good neighbour and caring for those in need.

A The parish church is the centre of local religious life

How the local church helps individual believers and the local area

The Bible calls the Church 'the body of Christ' and Christians believe that the Church is holy and belongs to God. The Church's mission is to preach the gospel and to make God's kingdom a reality in their own local community.

Each **local church** follows that mission. It also supports believers in following Jesus' teachings in their own lives, encouraging them to be good people. Local churches carry out their mission in various ways, by:

- offering the church as a community centre to bring local people together
- giving spiritual support to the sick
- praying for those in need
- supporting groups that campaign for justice and peace
- offering moral guidance
- telling others about Jesus (evangelism)
- **outreach** to children, the poor and the needy
- supporting young adults with advice on jobs, training, finance, and finding a home
- giving friendship and help to the elderly
- raising money for charity.

B Is it really the role of local churches to feed the poor?

STRETCH Should local churches be used just by believers or also by non-believers?

Ecumenism

There is a movement within the Church that tries to create unity and friendship between different Christian denominations. It is called **ecumenism**. Supporters say that closer union will lead to:

- tolerance of different ideas
- mutual understanding of the Christian faith
- less discrimination and conflict
- friendship among Christians.

C Pope Francis meets Archbishop Justin Welby and his wife at the Vatican in 2013

BUILD YOUR SKILLS

1 What do these terms mean, and why are they important? Parish, the local church, ecumenism.

2 a What are Christians being taught to do in these Bible verses?

> ‘To the elders among you [...] Be shepherds of God's flock that is under your care, watching over them – not because you must, but because you are willing, as God wants you to be; not pursuing dishonest gain, but eager to serve; not lording it over those entrusted to you, but being examples to the flock. And when the Chief Shepherd appears, you will receive the crown of glory that will never fade away.’
> *(1 Peter 5: 1–4)*

> ‘Always be prepared to give an answer to everyone who asks you to give the reason for the hope that you have.’
> *(1 Peter 3: 15)*

> ‘Whoever welcomes one of these little children in my name welcomes me.’
> *(Mark 9: 37)*

b How might a Christian put each of these teachings into practice today?

USEFUL TERMS

Ecumenism: a movement that tries to bring different Christian denominations closer together

Local church: a meeting place for local believers and the community of believers who gather there

Outreach: an activity to provide services to people in need

Parish: a community of local believers within a particular denomination

SUMMARY

- Parish churches are the centre of local religious life but they also welcome atheists.
- They preach the Christian faith and help the needy.
- They offer advice and special services for the important events in people's lives.
- The different denominations of the Christian Church are working together through ecumenism to create greater understanding with each other.

EXAM-STYLE QUESTIONS

a Outline **three** ways that the local church serves its local community. (3)

b Explain **two** reasons why ecumenism is important to Christians. (4)

3.8 The worldwide Church

What is the role of the Church in the worldwide community?

The Church exists in every nation and aims to have a positive spiritual impact on the world. Its roles include:

- representing Jesus on earth
- bringing the gospel to all people
- helping the poor, the sick, and the needy
- promoting friendships
- bringing together as a community all the people who want to know and love God.

The Church is important within the global community because it encourages peace and harmony between individuals and countries, and teaches and tries to set a good example of living a moral life. It also organises charity work, supports the work of its missionaries and helps Christians in need around the world.

The Church also has powerful influence in debates on:

- abortion
- injustice
- marriage
- moral issues
- political decisions
- poverty
- same-sex relationships.

SPECIFICATION FOCUS

The role and importance of the Church in the worldwide community: how and why it works for reconciliation and the problems faced by the persecuted Church; divergent Christian responses to teachings about charity, including 1 Corinthians 13 and Matthew 25: 31–46; the work of Christian Aid, what it does and why.

❛Wherever we see the Word of God purely preached and heard, there a church of God exists.❜
Theologian John Calvin (1509–1564)

A The world listens to South Africa's Archbishop Desmond Tutu, who was awarded the 1984 Nobel Peace Prize for his key role in fighting against racial discrimination in his homeland

What is reconciliation?

Reconciliation mends broken relationships, bringing peace and harmony between individuals, groups or countries. Today, the Church seeks to reconcile relationships around the world because Jesus taught, 'As I have loved you, so you must love one another' *(John 13: 34)* and because the Bible says:

> 'All this is from God, who reconciled us to himself through Christ and gave us the ministry of reconciliation.'
> *(2 Corinthians 5: 18)*

> **SUPPORT**
> Have you ever fallen out with someone? Did you make up? What steps were needed in order to 'reconcile' with them?

The Church brings together people of different, and often opposing, beliefs to help them reach a reconciliation. It offers prayer, friendship and advice, as well as financial help and expert practical help in difficult situations. Two examples are the Ecumenical Movement and the World Council of Churches.

Ecumenical Movement

Aims to bring Christians of different and opposing viewpoints together by:

- praying and seeking guidance
- arranging meetings to share viewpoints and situations
- getting churches and groups to work together
- holding conferences and events around the world.

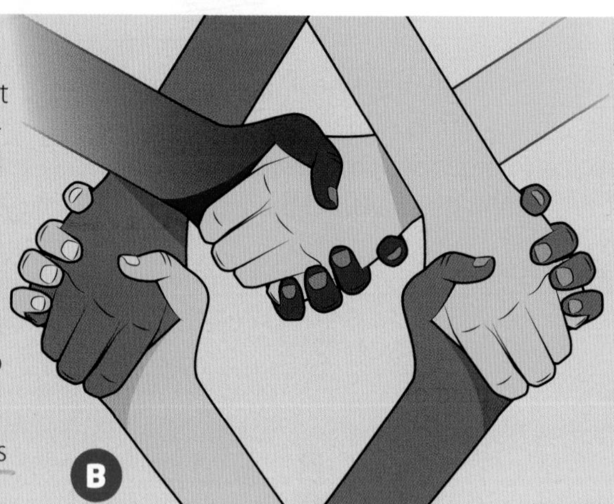

B

World Council of Churches

Seeks reconciliation and peace for people around the world by:

- organising days of prayer
- campaigning for peace and human rights
- responding to calls for help and support
- speaking out against oppression and terrorism
- supporting missionaries.

What is persecution?

Persecution is the ill-treatment of an individual or group, usually on the grounds of religion, politics or ethnicity. Another word for it is **oppression**. Globally, persecution happens on a daily basis. Members or groups within various different faiths have experienced persecution, but a minority who claim allegiance with a particular faith can also be persecutors themselves, often where two different belief systems collide. For example, there is a history of violence between Christian and Muslim groups in Nigeria, with atrocities carried out by both sides.

> **STRETCH**
> Do you think that people should always seek reconciliation? Are there some circumstances, such as persecution, where reconciliation seems impossible?

Global persecution of Christians is often referred to as 'the persecuted Church', and takes place in many countries, for instance China, North Korea, and India. According to the International Society for Human Rights, 80 per cent of all religious discrimination in the world is currently directed at Christians. It has also been estimated that 100,000 Christians die every year because of their faith. Former Chief Rabbi Jonathan Sacks told the House of Lords that the persecution of Christians is 'one of the crimes against humanity of our time'. However, very few

C Pakistani Christians mourn after hundreds of people are killed or injured during Easter celebrations in 2016

USEFUL TERMS

Charity: giving to those in need

Persecution: the ill-treatment of an individual or group, usually on the grounds of religion, politics or ethnicity

Reconciliation: restoring peace and friendship between individuals or groups

people in the wealthy countries of 'the West' know about this persecution. One victim said:

> 'Does anybody hear our cry? How many atrocities must we endure before somebody comes to our aid?'

Teachings about charity

Christians have a duty to help those in need. This is called **charity**. The Bible says that followers of Jesus must 'love your neighbour as yourself' *(Mark 12: 31)*, and that everything they own comes from God and that they look after it for him (see stewardship in 1.2).

> 'Go, sell everything you have and give it to the poor, and you will have treasure in heaven.'
> *(Mark 10: 21)*

Although this type of giving is central to Christian teaching, many Christians believe it is especially important to do it quietly. This is because Jesus said:

> 'Be careful not to practise your righteousness in front of others to be seen by them. If you do, you will have no reward from your Father in heaven [...] [Give your gifts] in secret. Then your Father, who sees what is done in secret, will reward you.'
> *(Matthew 6: 1, 4)*

D The Salvation Army is an international charitable organisation as well as a Church, whose mission includes 'serving suffering humanity'

St Paul teaches that giving to charity ought to be joyful, and that people should not be forced to give:

> ‘Each of you should give what you have decided in your heart to give, not reluctantly or under compulsion, for God loves a cheerful giver.’
> *(2 Corinthians 9: 7)*

One of Jesus' most powerful teachings on charity is the parable of the sheep and goats *(Matthew 25, 31–46)*. In it he tells believers that, whenever they give to the poor, they are giving to him:

> **‘... whatever you did for one of the least of these brothers and sisters of mine, you did for me.’**
> *(Matthew 25: 40)*

SUPPORT

Christians have a profound love and respect for Jesus, and in this teaching he is telling them to treat others with the same respect that they have for him.

The most important aspect of Christian charity is love:

> **‘If I give all I possess to the poor [...] but do not have love, I gain nothing.’**
> *(1 Corinthians 13: 3)*

STRETCH

Why is love so important for Christians giving to charity? Isn't the actual gift the most important thing?

Divergent Christian responses

Christians may respond in a variety of ways to these teachings. Some will give charity and tell no one that they have done it, whereas others will discuss it so as to encourage others to give. Often, Christians will ask God to help them to give joyfully, especially because giving involves a degree of sacrifice and it requires love and compassion. Many Christians will give regular financial gifts to the poor, but giving is not always financial: it can also involve time, effort, and skills dedicated to serving people in need.

Christian Aid

One of the ways believers, and non-believers, can help those in need is to donate to charities like Christian Aid. This is the official relief and development agency of 41 Churches. Much of the money donated to it comes from individual Christians and churches, particularly during Christian Aid Week.

Christian Aid works with local organisations around the world where the need is greatest, regardless of religion or race. It is founded on Christian principles of justice and fairness for all and seeks to obey Jesus' teaching to love one another. Its mission statement is:

> ‘Christian Aid insists the world can and must be swiftly changed to one where everyone can live a full life, free from poverty.’

E Christian Aid and partners distributing relief material in the Kathmandu Valley following the Nepal earthquake in May 2015

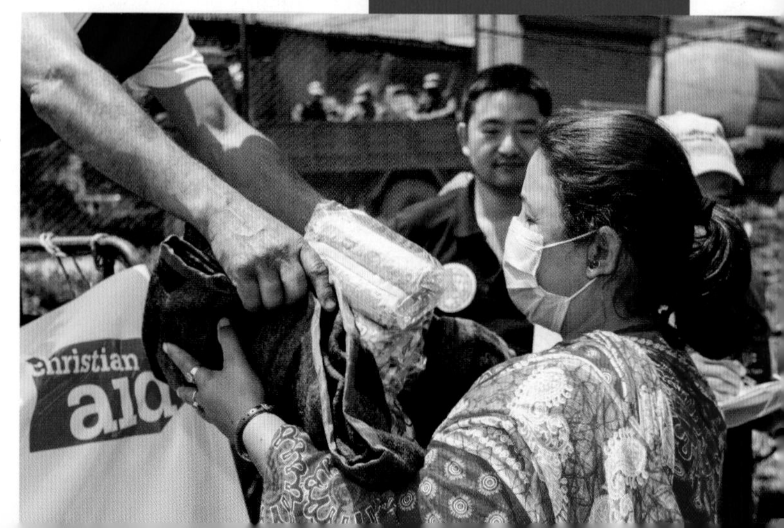

It aims to help the poor to help themselves and often uses the saying,

> 'Give a man a fish, feed him for a day; teach a man to fish, feed him for life.'

Christian Aid operates in three main ways:

- It gives immediate aid such as first aid, food, shelter, and clothing in times of disaster. In 2014, it gave emergency help during the famine in South Sudan and the Ebola disease outbreak in Sierra Leone, and in 2015 after the earthquake in Nepal.
- It gives long-term aid and education to help the poor feed themselves. For example, it has provided medical care, clean water, and farming equipment in many countries, including Ethiopia, Malawi and Afghanistan.
- It runs political campaigns. In 2012, it organised marches in London against climate change and for more provision for the poor.

Christian Aid also works for reconciliation, defends the poor against the rich and powerful, works to end oppressive debt, and campaigns for justice and human rights.

BUILD YOUR SKILLS

1 Copy and complete the following table for the Church in the worldwide community.

	What does it mean?	How does it impact the Church?
Reconciliation		
Persecution		
Charity		

2 'Charity begins at home.' Is it right to give charity and financial aid to overseas countries when there is poverty and need in the UK?
  a How would a Christian answer this and why?
  b What is your own view?

3 Find out more about the work of Christian Aid. Can you link what they say and do to specific Christian teachings?

STRETCH

SUMMARY

- The Christian Church seeks to have a positive impact on the world.
- It preaches the gospel all around the world.
- It helps the needy and tries to influence debate on many global issues.
- It works for reconciliation.
- Many Christians around the world are persecuted for their faith.
- The Bible teaches that Christians must give charity to those in need and Christian Aid is the official Church charity for carrying out that work.

EXAM-STYLE QUESTIONS

b Explain **two** ways that Christian Aid works to relieve poverty. (4)

c Explain **two** reasons why giving to charity is important to Christians. In your answer you must refer to a source of wisdom and authority. (5)

Revision

BUILD YOUR SKILLS

Look at the list of 'I can' statements below and think carefully about how confident you are. Use the following code to rate each of the statements. Be honest!

Green – very confident. What is your evidence for this?

Orange – quite confident. What is your target? Be specific.

Red – not confident. What is your target? Be specific.

A self-assessment revision checklist is available on *Kerboodle*

I can…

- Describe the different ways that Christians worship, including liturgical, non-liturgical and individual, and explain when and why each form might be used
- Explain different Christian attitudes towards liturgical and non-liturgical forms of worship including reference to different denominations
- Explain what sacraments are and why they are important
- Describe the meaning and celebration of baptism and the Eucharist in at least two denominations, including reference to a source of wisdom and authority
- Describe different Christian attitudes towards the use and number of sacraments in Orthodox, Catholic, and Protestant traditions
- Give examples of different kinds of prayer, with reference to a source of wisdom and authority
- Explain when each type of prayer might be used and why
- Describe different Christian attitudes towards the importance of each type of prayer for Christians today
- Explain what pilgrimage is and why people go on pilgrimages
- Describe the activities associated with different Christian pilgrimages
- Explain different Christian teachings about whether pilgrimage is important for Christians today, with reference to Catholic and Protestant understandings
- Explain the origins and importance of Advent and Christmas
- Explain the origins and importance of Holy Week and Easter, with reference to a source of wisdom and authority
- Explain the meaning of the terms mission and evangelism
- Explain the history and purpose of missionary and evangelistic work in the Church, with reference to a source of wisdom and authority
- Describe some different ways that this work is put into practice by the Church
- Describe Christian attitudes to why evangelistic work is important for the Church and individual Christians
- Explain what the local church does in the local community and why, including reference to a source of wisdom and authority
- Describe the impact the local church has on the individual believer and the local area
- Explain the role and importance of the Church in the worldwide community
- Explain why the Church works for reconciliation
- Describe the problems faced by the persecuted Church
- Give different Christian responses to teachings about charity, with reference to a source of wisdom and authority
- Describe the work of Christian Aid – what it does and why.

Exam practice

On these exam practice pages you will see example answers for each of the exam question types: **a**, **b**, **c**, and **d**. You can find out more about these on pages 6–11.

• Question 'a'

*Question **a** is AO1 – this tests your knowledge and understanding.*

(a) Outline **three** Christian sacraments. (3)

Student response

Baptism, bread and wine, becoming a priest

WHAT WENT WELL

This student can identify three different types of sacrament.

Improved student response

Baptism, formally becoming a member of the Christian Church.

Eucharist, a re-enactment of the last supper.

Holy Orders, becoming a priest, deacon or bishop in Catholic and Orthodox Churches.

HOW TO IMPROVE

To make the response clearer and gain full marks the student should use the religious names for the sacraments and explain each one. See the 'improved student response' opposite for suggested corrections.

Over to you! Give yourself three minutes on the clock and have a go at answering this question. Remember, this question type requires you to provide three facts or short ideas: you don't need to explain them or express any opinions.

• Question 'b'

*Question **b** is AO1 – this tests your knowledge and understanding.*

(b) Explain **two** reasons why prayer is important to Christians. (4)

Student response

Prayer is important to Christians because it is a way of communicating with God. People can pray for different things, for example, to ask for something.

WHAT WENT WELL

This is a low-level response with two vague and basic reasons given. The student correctly identifies that prayer is a way of communicating with God.

Improved student response

Prayer is important to Christians because it is a way of communicating with God. Through prayer Christians can give thanks and praise to God but also ask for things on behalf of themselves or others.

Prayer is important to Christians because Jesus taught people to pray using the Lord's Prayer and people like to follow his example. In addition, using formal prayers or words from Church history help Christians to feel a shared sense of belief and unity making this form of prayer important for Christians.

HOW TO IMPROVE

The reasons given are basic and are not developed. For a high level response students should explain why prayer is important to individual Christians, using examples of how they pray and the types of prayer they use. See the 'improved student response' opposite for suggested corrections.

Over to you! Give yourself four minutes on the clock and have a go at answering this question. Remember, in order to 'explain' something, you need to **develop** your points. See page 9 for a reminder of how to do this.

• Question 'c'

*Question **c** is A01 – this tests your knowledge and understanding.*

> (c) Explain **two** reasons why giving to charity is important to Christians. In your answer you must refer to a source of wisdom and authority. (5)

Student response

The Bible says that Christians must give charity to those in need. Supporting charities is a good thing and the Christian Church seeks to have a positive impact on the world.

WHAT WENT WELL

This student understands that charity is important and the global Church has a responsibility to help others.

HOW TO IMPROVE

The link between helping others by giving to charity and Christian teachings on charity could be clearer. Has the student included a source of wisdom and authority? See the 'improved student response' opposite for suggested corrections.

Improved student response

Giving to charity is important to Christians because the Bible says that Christians must give charity to those in need. In Jesus' teaching of the parable of the sheep and the goats Jesus says that if we help others, in fact we are helping him, showing that charity to others is important: "whatever you did for one of the least of these brothers and sisters of mine, you did for me" (Matthew 25: 40).

Secondly, Christians are taught that the most charitable act is love and often Christians do not give financially to charity but will give time, effort and skills because supporting charities is a good thing and the Christian Church seeks to have a positive impact on the world.

Over to you! Give yourself five minutes on the clock and have a go at answering this question. Remember, you need to write two developed points, one of which needs to be supported by a source of wisdom and authority.

• Question 'd'

*Question **d** is A02 – this tests your ability to evaluate. Some 'd' questions also carry an extra three marks for spelling, punctuation and grammar.*

> **In this question, 3 of the marks awarded will be for your spelling, punctuation and grammar and your use of specialist terminology.**
>
> *(d) 'Every Christian should go on a pilgrimage.' Evaluate this statement considering arguments for and against. In your response you should:
> - refer to Christian teachings
> - refer to different Christian points of view
> - reach a justified conclusion. (15)

Student response

Christians have been going on pilgrimiges for centuries, and today pilgrimige is still popular. Pilgrimige can increase a Christian's faith, help them feel closer to God, and may bring about religious experiences.

I would agree with the claim that every Christian should go on a pilgrimige, because it's a spiritual journey towards God. Many popular sites of pilgrimige –

for instance Jerusalem – are visited by Christians and it could be argued that Christians should go to Jerusalem because Jesus himself did this.

However, not all Christians place emphasis on pilgrimige. It might be encouraged as a special opportunity to pray and reflect, but it's not considered to be central to living the Christian life. These Christians might choose to focus on other aspects of their faith instead.

In conclusion, whilst pilgrimige would be very beneficial to all Christians, it's not possible to say that all Christians should go on a pilgrimige. It's not a religious requirement, and in some churches it's not a significant part of the Christian life.

WHAT WENT WELL

This is a mid-level response. The student understands that they must give two opposing sides of the argument and reach a conclusion. They explain both arguments and present a conclusion.

HOW TO IMPROVE

This student has consistently misspelt the word 'pilgrimage', which would cost them marks. To achieve a high-level answer, the student would need to be more specific when referring to different Christian viewpoints, and provide more detail on Christian teachings. See the 'improved student response' opposite for suggested corrections.

Improved student response

Christians have been going on pilgrimages for centuries, and today pilgrimage is still popular. Pilgrimage can increase a Christian's faith, help them feel closer to God, and may bring about religious experiences.

A member of the Catholic Church could agree with the claim that every Christian should go on a pilgrimage, because the Catholic Church teaches about its importance in the Catechism: 'Pilgrimages evoke our earthly journey toward heaven' (CCC 2691). In other words, pilgrimage is a spiritual journey towards God.

Pilgrimage is important in Protestant churches too, and many popular sites of pilgrimage – for instance Jerusalem and Walsingham – are visited by all denominations. Walsingham, for instance, has Catholic, Anglican, and Orthodox shrines. It could be argued that all Christians should go on a pilgrimage to Jerusalem because Jesus himself did this at the age of twelve and said that he had to be in his Father's house (Luke 2: 49). Pilgrimage can allow Christians to walk in the very footsteps of Jesus, or a saint. Pilgrimage is spiritually important because the pilgrim can, for a moment, be where Jesus or a saint was, see what they saw, and experience what the world was like for them – it makes it special for the pilgrim and something which they will never forget.

However, not all Protestant churches place emphasis on pilgrimage. It might be encouraged as a special opportunity to pray and reflect, but it's not considered to be central to living the Christian life. These Christians might choose to focus on other aspects of their faith instead, for example prayer, Bible study or evangelism – all of which bring Christians closer to God in an everyday way which fits into their lives.

In conclusion, whilst pilgrimage would be very beneficial to all Christians, it's not possible to say that all Christians should go on a pilgrimage. It's not a religious requirement, and in some churches it's not a significant part of the Christian life.

Over to you! Give yourself 15 minutes on the clock and have a go at answering this question. Remember to refer back to the original statement in your writing when you give different points of view, and make sure you cover each of the bullet points given in the question. Allow three minutes to check your spelling, punctuation and grammar and use of specialist terminology.

BUILD YOUR SKILLS

In your exams, you'll need to make sure you use religious terminology correctly. Do you know the meaning of the following important terms for this topic?

Chapter 4: Matters of Life and Death

4.1 Origins and value of the universe

SPECIFICATION FOCUS

Christian teachings about the origins and value of the universe: scientific explanations for the origins of the universe and Christian responses to them, including the work of Georges Lemaître; the value of the universe in Christian teaching; Christian responses to the possible view that the universe can be used as a commodity, including interpretations of Genesis 1–2.

What are the scientific explanations for the origins of the universe?

What are the origins of the universe? Has it always existed, or did it begin at a particular point in time? These questions have been asked for centuries. In 1927, a Belgian Catholic priest called Georges Lemaître posed a scientific theory that would form the basis of what is now called the **Big Bang theory**. Lemaître proposed that the universe is expanding, and may have begun at a single, original point. The Big Bang theory has been developed and tested further by scientists and it is the most widely held theory about the origins of the universe today. The theory suggests that:

- 13.7 billion years ago the matter in the universe was concentrated into one small, dense, high temperature point
- This expanded, and after the initial expansion it began to cool, allowing for the formation of particles and atoms
- Clouds of these elements went on to form stars and galaxies
- When the Earth had cooled, life began to develop.

The Big Bang theory is based on scientific evidence. One of the most important pieces of evidence is called Hubble's Law, which measures the rate at which objects in deep space are travelling away from the Earth.

The Big Bang theory has been seen by many as proof against the existence of God, because it offers an explanation of how the universe was created.

A This photograph, taken by the Hubble Telescope, is of the farthest edge of the universe – more than 12 billion light years away. How might this influence belief in God?

Christian responses

Christians believe that the universe was created by God, though there are different views among Christians as to whether the biblical accounts of creation should be taken literally or metaphorically (see 1.2).

Some Christians would reject the Big Bang theory for the following reasons:

- Science is always changing and may not have the whole picture – for example, early scientists were once convinced that the Earth was flat.
- The Bible is the word of God, and the story of creation should therefore be taken literally. The story describes God creating the Earth in six days, which is not compatible with the Big Bang theory.

However, many Christians believe that the Big Bang theory is compatible with the belief that God created the universe. When he proposed his theory of an expanding universe, Georges Lemaître did not think that his theory proved or disproved the existence of God. He thought that it left the question open to be decided in other ways:

> ‘As far as I can see, such a theory remains entirely outside any metaphysical or religious question.’
> *(Lemaître)*

Many Christians would agree with Lemaître's view that science and religion are attempting to answer two different questions. They would argue that – since the biblical account of creation is metaphorical – it is entirely possible that God was the cause of the Big Bang.

Why is the universe valuable for Christians?

Christians believe that the universe has value because:

- **God created the universe and continues to sustain it:** '[…] all things have been created through him and for him. He is before all things, and in him all things hold together.' *(Colossians 1: 16–17)*
- **The universe reflects God's love and power:** 'When I consider your heavens, the work of your fingers […] what is mankind that you are mindful of them, human beings that you care for them?' *(Psalm 8: 3–4)*
- **It is given to humanity as a gift for them to steward** (see 4.8)**:** 'God blessed them and said to them, "Be fruitful and increase in number; fill the earth and subdue it. Rule over the fish in the sea and the birds in the sky and over every living creature that moves on the ground."' *(Genesis 1: 28)*.

The universe as a commodity

Christians believe that the universe is a gift from God. In *Genesis 1–2*, it is clear that humans are given a special importance in creation, and in *Genesis 1: 28* they are commanded to 'rule' over it. Some would suggest, therefore, that the universe is a **commodity**. In other words, it is something that can be used to satisfy wants and needs.

USEFUL TERMS

Big Bang theory: a scientific theory about the origin of the universe which suggests that the universe is expanding away from a single point, a process which started around 13.7 billion years ago

Commodity: a useful or valuable thing which satisfies particular wants or needs

B Georges Lemaître

C Does *Genesis 1: 28* give humans the right to exploit animals and the world's resources in any way they choose?

Some would argue that humans are entitled to exploit the world's resources in any way they wish. Most Christians, however, have environmental and ethical concerns over human treatment of the Earth and its resources, and believe that humans should look after the world. These Christians may be concerned about viewing the universe purely as a commodity, because of the risk of developing a selfish attitude towards it. They would argue that the universe is to be enjoyed, but responsibly and sustainably.

BUILD YOUR SKILLS

1. Draw and annotate a diagram to explain the Big Bang theory.
2. Describe two different Christian responses to the Big Bang theory. How convincing do you find each one? Explain your reasons.
3. 'Resources in the world are there to be used. When they're gone, they're gone.' Make a list of arguments for and against this statement, including any Christian viewpoints.
4. How might Christians believe that both God and the Big Bang are real? **STRETCH**

SUMMARY

- The Big Bang theory is the most widely held scientific theory about the origin of the universe.
- Some Christians reject the Big Bang theory, but others believe that religion and science are compatible.
- Christians believe that the universe has value because it was designed and created by God.

EXAM-STYLE QUESTIONS

a. Outline **three** features of a scientific explanation for the origin of the universe. (3)

c. Explain **two** reasons why Christians believe the universe has value. In your answer you must refer to a source of wisdom and authority. (5)

4.2 Sanctity of life

SPECIFICATION FOCUS

Christian teachings about the sanctity of life: why human life is holy; how the Bible can be interpreted to show life as special, including reference to being created in the image of God as shown in Genesis 1–3; the importance of sanctity of life for Christians today.

What is sanctity of life?

The principle of the **sanctity of life** is an important theme in Christian discussion about many moral issues. Sanctity of life means that life is sacred, or holy, and set apart for God's purposes. Christians believe that God has a very special relationship with human beings because they are made in his image and have responsibility over the rest of creation. Christians believe that human life must be treated with special care, and decisions about life and death must be made very carefully. Christians believe that human life is intrinsically valuable – this means that it is not valuable because of what humans can do or what their personality is like, they are valuable and important simply because of what they are – human beings made in the image of God.

Christians do not believe that humans are perfect – this is not why life is sacred. Christians believe humans were created perfectly by God but because they sinned, that perfection was spoiled. However, humans are still like God, and that likeness means that human life is always to be treated with dignity and respect.

Can you explain what **sanctity of life** means in your own words?

What does the Bible teach about the value of human life?

The Bible teaches that human beings were created by God and are therefore valuable to him. Christians learn the following from the Bible:

- **Humans are made in God's image:** 'So God created mankind in his own image, in the image of God he created them: male and female he created them' *(Genesis 1: 27)*.
- **God breathed life into humans:** 'Then the Lord God formed a man from the dust of the ground and breathed into his nostrils the breath of life, and the man became a living being' *(Genesis 2: 7)*.
- **God planned each person before they existed:** 'Before I formed you in the womb I knew you, before you were born I set you apart' *(Jeremiah 1: 5)*.
- **Every part of a human's life was designed by God:** 'For you created my inmost being; you knit me together in my mother's womb. I praise you because I am fearfully and wonderfully made' *(Psalm 139: 13–14)*.
- **The human body was designed to be a special dwelling for the Holy Spirit:** 'Do you not know that your bodies are temples of the Holy Spirit, who is in you, whom you have received from God? You are not your own [...] therefore honour God with your bodies' *(1 Corinthians 6: 19–20)*.

Genesis 1: 27 describes humans as being made in the image of God, but does not describe any other living things in the same way. For this reason, most Christians believe that the principle of the sanctity of life belongs only to humans. Other Christians may

A How would you explain the idea of the sanctity of life?

disagree with this on the grounds that all life is precious – animals, birds, fish, and insects, as well as humans. However, in *Genesis 9: 4* humans are given authority by God to eat animals: 'Everything that lives and moves about will be food for you. Just as I gave you the green plants, I now give you everything.'

Humans are commanded not to murder *(Exodus 20: 13)*, and are told that they will be accountable for all human bloodshed. For this reason murder carried the death penalty in biblical times and still does in many countries today.

> ❛Whoever sheds human blood, by humans shall their blood be shed; for in the image of God has God made mankind.❜
> *(Genesis 9: 6)*

The teaching of the Catholic Church states:

> ❛God alone is the Lord of life [...] no one can under any circumstance claim for himself the right directly to destroy an innocent human being.❜
> *(Catechism of the Catholic Church, 2258)*

Why is the sanctity of life important for Christians today?

Sanctity of life is very important for Christians today for several reasons.

- Sanctity of life means that God cares for humans. A relationship with God – made possible because of the death and resurrection (see 4.5) of Jesus – is central to a Christian's faith.
- Christians believe God loves all people unconditionally, and therefore all humans are held to be equally important. This means that all humans are entitled to dignity and respect, including those who are young, unwell, or elderly.
- Sanctity of life means that important decisions about life and death – for example abortion and euthanasia – are taken very seriously (see 4.4 and 4.7).
- Some Christians argue that human life is sacred from conception (see 4.4) – this means that they are concerned about what happens to embryos and unborn babies, and not just about those who are born.

SUMMARY

- Christians believe God created humanity in his own image. This means that human life is intrinsically valuable.
- The Old and New Testaments make clear statements about the value of life.
- Sanctity of life is usually considered to apply only to humans and helps Christians make decisions about life and death matters.

USEFUL TERMS

Sanctity of life: the belief that life is created by God and made holy by him

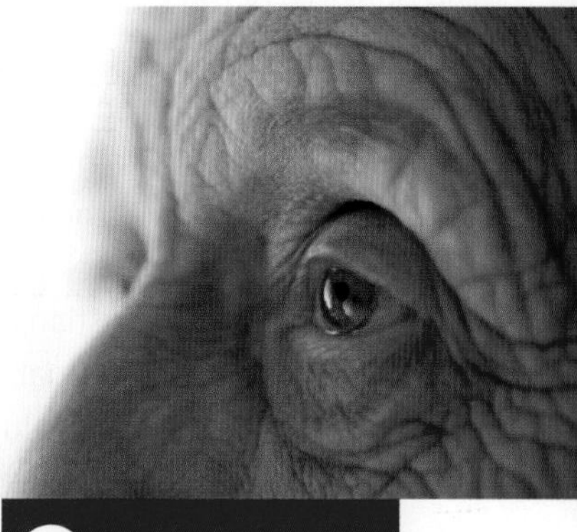

B For Christians, all life stages are sacred

STRETCH

Find out about the legal status given to embryos created in a laboratory. Consider whether this means that the law sees them as having sanctity of life.

BUILD YOUR SKILLS

1. Explain why Christians believe human life is holy. Refer to more than one Christian teaching.
2. Why is the sanctity of life important for Christians today? Explain which reasons you think are the most important and why.

EXAM-STYLE QUESTIONS

a. Outline **three** reasons why Christians believe that life is sacred. (3)
b. Explain **two** Christian teachings about the sanctity of life. (4)

4.3 Origins and value of human life

SPECIFICATION FOCUS

Christian responses to scientific and non-religious explanations about the origins and value of human life, such as evolution and survival of the fittest, including Special Agenda IV Diocesan Synod motions on compatibility of science and Christian belief (Diocese of Manchester); the significance of the responses to scientific and non-religious explanations, such as evolution and survival of the fittest, for Christians today.

What are scientific and non-religious explanations about the origins and value of human life?

One of the most important scientific explanations of life on Earth is the theory of **evolution** by natural selection, which is attributed to Charles Darwin and Alfred Russel Wallace, and was published by Darwin in his book *The Origin of Species* (1859). Darwin was a naturalist, which means that he travelled and studied animals and plants by observing them and conducting experiments. His theory proposes that all living things are descended from common ancestors and that different species have evolved over millions of years across many generations:

- Darwin claimed that evolution was driven by natural selection. On his travels, he noticed that members of the same species in different locations were slightly different. For example, he found that a particular species of finch had different shaped beaks and other features – features which were suited to the food that was available in that location (see image **A**).
- Darwin observed, therefore, that species can change gradually over time, to suit their particular environment.
- Central to this process is **survival of the fittest**. This means that those individuals who have features that are best suited to their environment are the most likely to survive and pass on their genes.
- The features that allowed these individuals to survive were passed on to the next generation, and so on.

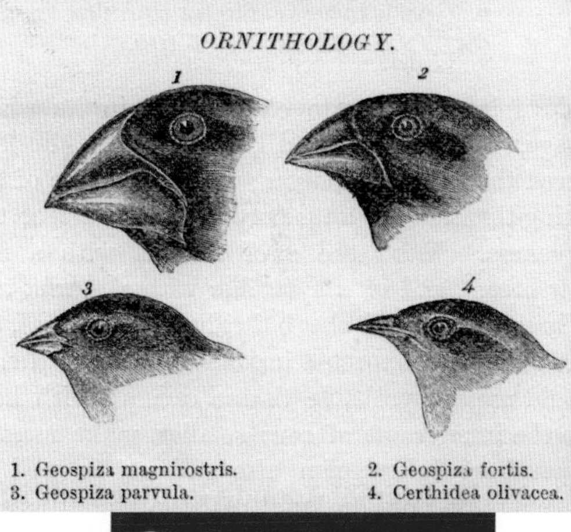

A Darwin noticed variations in the beaks of finches on adjacent islands. He concluded that finches had changed over time.

B Evolutionists believe that humans share a common ancestry with apes

The value of human life

The theory of evolution suggests that human beings have also evolved over time, and share a common ancestry with apes. This idea could support one non-religious view that human beings have comparable value to other forms of life on Earth – in other words, they are no more important than animals or plants. However, some non-religious people might disagree with this on the basis that human beings seem to have a superior ability to reason and feel.

> **STRETCH**
> Which would you choose to support: a charity which helps vulnerable people, or a charity which helps vulnerable animals? Does your answer have anything to do with the value of human life? Explain your views.

Christian responses

As we have seen in 4.1, Christian responses to scientific ideas often depend on whether or not they believe those ideas to be compatible with the Bible.

Christians who reject the theory of evolution would do so because the Bible says that God created humankind, and that he created them in his own image. To claim that human beings share a common ancestry with apes, and that they evolved over a long period of time, contradicts the Bible and undermines the importance that God gives to human beings.

Other Christians believe that the theory of evolution is compatible with the Bible. They would argue that God can use any method for creation, including evolution, and that God can still be personally involved in the process of evolution, even if it took place over millions of years. For these Christians, the following core principles are still compatible with science:

- God is responsible for bringing something out of nothing and order out of chaos
- God's creative work is perfect and purposeful
- there is a harmony between all aspects of creation
- human beings are given special responsibilities and callings.

One area of disagreement is related to the sanctity of life (see 4.2). Christians believe that human beings are particularly valuable to God. They believe they should care for and steward creation, but human life is believed to be holy. This view is not shared by non-religious people.

USEFUL TERMS

Evolution: the process by which different species have developed from earlier forms

General Synod: the national group within the Church of England that debates issues relating to Christian belief and practice

Survival of the fittest: the idea that members of a species that are best suited to an environment survive

The Special Agenda IV Diocesan Synod

In 2010 the **General Synod** of the Church of England agreed that the divine design in the universe is achieved by God through the way in which the laws of the universe work and the process of evolution. The Synod concluded that mainstream science and Christian thought were entirely compatible. The thinking behind this is that Genesis offers a general account rather describing an actual event; in effect, it is a story to communicate an idea.

> **SUPPORT**
> This suggests that Christians can accept the theory of evolution because it does not go against the Bible.

The significance of Christian responses to scientific and non-religious explanations

Many Christians believe it is important to respond to scientific and non-religious explanations because:

- there is strong evidence to support scientific explanations, and ignoring them suggests that Christians are not willing or able to respond to challenges
- Christians need to consider how scientific and religious views may be compatible
- Christians can learn and be 'enriched' by shared knowledge:

> 'The question about the origins of the world and of man has been the object of many scientific studies which have splendidly enriched our knowledge of the age and dimensions of the cosmos, the development of life-forms and the appearance of man. These discoveries invite us to even greater admiration for the greatness of the Creator, prompting us to give him thanks for all his works and for the understanding and wisdom he gives to scholars and researchers.'
> *(Catechism of the Catholic Church, 283)*

> 'God didn't produce a ready-made world. The Creator has done something cleverer than this, making a world able to make itself.'
> *(John Polkinghorne)*

C John Polkinghorne is a Christian Anglican priest and a physicist. What do you think this quotation from him means?

BUILD YOUR SKILLS

1. Explain the theory of evolution in your own words. Include the phrases 'natural selection' and 'survival of the fittest'.
2. Create a table which contains Christian arguments for and against the theory of evolution.
3. What are the implications of evolution for the sanctity of life? Refer to a range of viewpoints in your answer. STRETCH

SUMMARY

- Evolution is a scientific theory which suggests that different species, including humans, have developed from earlier forms.
- Christians disagree about scientific and non-religious explanations of the origins of human life.
- Many Christians believe it is important to respond to the challenges posed by these explanations.

EXAM-STYLE QUESTIONS

b. Explain **two** Christian responses to scientific explanations about the origins of human life. (4)

d. 'Human life created itself.' Evaluate this statement considering arguments for and against. In your response you should:
   - refer to Christian teachings
   - refer to different Christian points of view
   - refer to non-religious points of view
   - reach a justified conclusion. (12)

4.4 Abortion

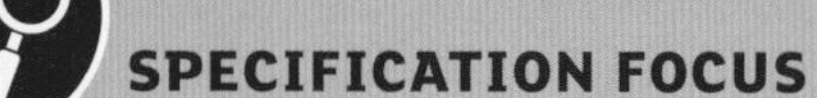

SPECIFICATION FOCUS

Implications of the value and sanctity of life for the issue of abortion: the nature of abortion; divergent Christian pro-life and pro-choice teachings about abortion, including reference to Humanae Vitae; non-religious (including atheist and Humanist) arguments surrounding its use, including the application of ethical theories, such as situation ethics, and Christian responses to them.

What is abortion?

Abortion is the deliberate ending of a pregnancy by surgical or medical means. Abortions were legalised in the UK under the Abortion Act 1967 (amended 1990), which allows abortion up to the twenty-fourth week of pregnancy, as long as two doctors agree on at least one of the following conditions:

- the pregnancy puts at risk the physical or mental health of the woman or her existing children
- the abortion will prevent serious permanent injury to the woman
- continuing the pregnancy puts the woman's life at risk
- there is a high risk that the child would be severely disabled.

Later abortions are permitted only if the woman's life is at risk or a serious disability is detected.

Abortion is one of the most important moral issues in the developed world and it is not just a religious concern. The issue revolves around whether the foetus (or 'unborn child') counts as a person.

- Those who claim that a foetus is a person may argue that:
  'It is wrong to kill a person.
  A foetus is a person.
  Therefore abortion is wrong.'
- Those who claim it is not yet a person may argue that:
  'It is wrong to kill a person.
  A foetus is not yet a person.
  Therefore abortion is not wrong.'

The key question is about when human life begins.

STRETCH

Look at the website of the Society for the Protection of the Unborn Child for greater understanding of why some people are opposed to abortion.

Look at the website of Abortion Rights, the national pro-choice campaign, to understand why some people support the right to abortion.

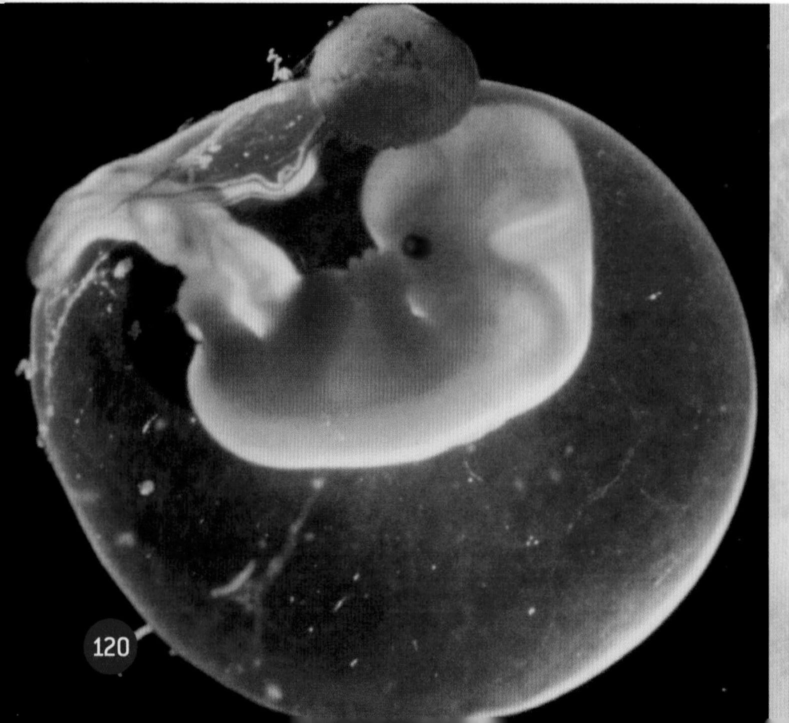

A Should a foetus be considered a person? Should it have the same rights as a baby? Discuss your views with a partner.

The debate about when life begins often refers to particular stages in the development of a foetus. This table summarises the changes a foetus goes through before birth.

Conception	**The sperm and egg fertilise**
0–5 weeks	The fertilised egg begins as a single cell, but begins to divide to form more than 100 cells – called an embryo. From 4 weeks the nervous system is developing, and the foundations for all major organs are in place.
6–8 weeks	From 6 weeks the heart is formed and can begin beating. Arms and legs, eyes and ears develop. The embryo is now known as a 'foetus'.
9–12 weeks	During these weeks, the foetus becomes fully formed. Its organs, muscles and limbs are formed, and it moves in the womb.
13–20 weeks	The foetus grows and matures, and organs begin to work. The face begins to look much more human. Fingernails and toenails are growing.
12–24 weeks *24 weeks is the legal limit for an abortion in the UK*	The foetus has a sleeping and waking cycle. Towards the end of this stage, the foetus has a chance of surviving outside the womb.
25–28 weeks	The foetus responds to touch and sound and moves vigorously. By the end of this stage the foetus may weigh 1kg and be fully formed.
29–36 weeks	The foetus' bones are hardening, and the foetus begins to move into position for birth.
37–40 weeks	The foetus is 'full term', and becomes ready to be born.

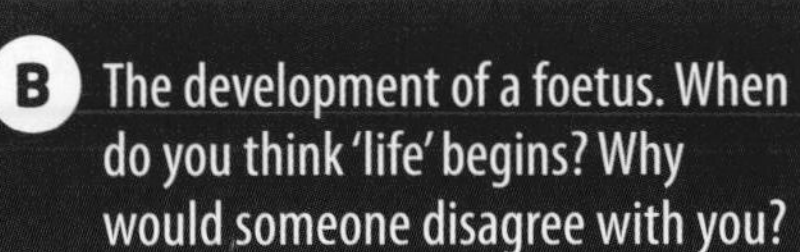
B The development of a foetus. When do you think 'life' begins? Why would someone disagree with you?

How do Christians view abortion?

The Catholic Church and most evangelical Protestants are **pro-life**. They oppose abortion on the grounds that life is sacred (the sanctity of life principle – see 4.2). They may argue that:

- life begins at **conception**
- the foetus is created in the image of God
- every human being has the right to life
- God has a plan for every human life: 'For you created my inmost being: you knit me together in my mother's womb' *(Psalm 139: 13)*
- abortion is murder, which is forbidden in the Bible (*Exodus 20: 13*).

> 'Human life must be respected and protected absolutely from the moment of conception. From the first moment of his existence, a human being must be recognized as having the rights of a person – among which is the inviolable right of every innocent being to life.'
> *(Catechism of the Catholic Church, 2270)*

USEFUL TERMS

Abortion: ending a pregnancy by deliberately removing a foetus by surgical or medical means

Conception: the moment when a sperm fertilises an egg, creating an embryo that can develop into a baby

Pro-choice: holding the belief that the mother should be able to choose whether to have an abortion

Pro-life: holding the belief that the foetus has a right to life

Situation ethics: ethical decisions made according to the specific context of the decision

The Catholic Church condemned abortion in the Papal Encyclical *Humanae Vitae* in 1968 as a means of controlling or preventing birth. Pope Paul VI wrote:

> ‘We are obliged once more to declare that the direct interruption of the generative process already begun and, above all, all direct abortion, even for therapeutic reasons, are to be absolutely excluded as lawful means of regulating the number of children.’
> *(Humanae Vitae, 14)*

C Pope Paul VI

The Church of England and some non-conformist churches are also opposed to abortion, but believe it may, under some circumstances, be the most compassionate option.

> ‘The Church of England combines strong opposition to abortion with a recognition that there can be – strictly limited – conditions under which it may be morally preferable to any available alternative.’
> *(Abortion, Church of England)*

> ‘The reasons for requesting abortion are many and complex and not always a result of human frailty. Whilst abortion may, in certain circumstances be seen as necessary, it is always regrettable and every effort should be made to reduce the need for recourse to it.’
> *(Methodist Statement on Abortion, 1976, updated 2010)*

> ‘The Synod has not attempted to resolve all the dilemmas which arise in this area, such as when the unborn child has been conceived as a result of rape or the foetus may be known to be at risk of serious handicap. Anglicans will be agreed on the need to have regard to ‘compassion for the mother and a proper responsibility for the life of the unborn child’ but they may come to different conclusions about the proper course of action in particular cases.’
> *(Abortion – A Briefing Paper, Church of England, 2005)*

D Pro-choice and pro-life campaigners

Some more liberal Christians would say they are **pro-choice**, and may give the following reasons for this:

- Jesus taught his followers to act with love and compassion
- Religion sometimes allows the sanctity of life to be broken, such as during war
- It is not clear that life begins at conception.

What are the non-religious arguments about abortion?

Like Christians, non-religious people could be pro-life or pro-choice, but their arguments would not be religious ones. They might argue:

Pro-choice	Pro-life
A foetus is not a person until it can survive outside the womb, so abortions before 24 weeks are not taking a life.	Every foetus has the potential for life. Thanks to modern medicine, babies can survive outside the womb at younger and younger ages.
A woman should have the right to choose what to do with her own body.	The woman's right shouldn't outweigh the rights of the foetus.
If a baby will not be wanted when it is born, it is better for it not to be born at all.	Adoption is an alternative to abortion. The baby could be happy with a different family.

Situation ethics is an ethical theory which suggests that decisions should be made based on what the most loving thing to do is, in the situation. A situation ethicist may be pro-life or pro-choice in different circumstances. They would carefully consider the situation and decide what action would best suit everyone. Most Christians would disagree with this method of decision-making, and would instead make decisions based on what they believe to be right according to the Bible, other Christian teachings, and their own conscience.

'There is not one, correct humanist view on abortion [...] As long as abortion is needed as a last resort, most humanists would agree that society should provide safe legal facilities. The alternatives, which would inevitably include illegal abortions, are far worse.'
(British Humanist Association)

BUILD YOUR SKILLS

1. Read the non-religious arguments for and against abortion. How would different Christians respond to each one? Refer to Christian teachings.
2. 'Abortion is sometimes the most compassionate option'.
   a. How would the following people respond to this statement? A Catholic, a Methodist, a pro-choice atheist, a situation ethicist.
   b. Write a mini conclusion, including which view(s) are most convincing and why.
3. Read the quotation from the British Humanist Association on this page.
   a. What are the 'alternatives' they mention?
   b. What do you think of this as an argument for the legalisation of abortion?

SUMMARY

- Abortion is the deliberate ending of a pregnancy by removing the foetus from the womb
- The problem of abortion revolves around the issue of when human life begins.
- Abortions are legal in the UK under certain circumstances.
- Many Christians oppose abortion on sanctity of life grounds; others are more flexible on grounds of compassion.
- Non-religious people might be pro-choice or pro-life.

EXAM-STYLE QUESTIONS

a. Outline **three** reasons why a Christian might oppose abortion. (3)

d. 'Abortion is always wrong, whatever the circumstances.' Evaluate this statement considering arguments for and against. In your response you should:
- refer to Christian teachings
- refer to different Christian points of view
- refer to non-religious points of view
- refer to relevant ethical arguments
- reach a justified conclusion. (12)

4.5 Life after death

SPECIFICATION FOCUS

Christian teachings and beliefs about life after death: Christian teachings and beliefs that support the existence of a life after death, including the resurrection of Jesus and Ephesians 2: 1–10; divergent Christian and non-religious arguments for life after death (including remembered lives, paranormal, logic, reward, comfort and meeting loved ones who have passed on); the significance of belief in life after death for Christians.

Christian beliefs and teachings about life after death are covered in detail in 1.6.

How do Christian teachings and beliefs support the existence of a life after death?

Christians believe in the existence of life after death because:

- the Bible promises an afterlife, for example, 'And God raised us up with Christ and seated us with him in the heavenly realms in Christ Jesus' *(Ephesians 2: 6)*
- if God is eternal, and he created life to have purpose and significance, then surely he would want human beings to continue to live beyond the grave
- the **resurrection** of Jesus is a guarantee of life after death for all those who believe in him: 'But if it is preached that Christ has been raised from the dead, how can some of you say that there is no resurrection of the dead?' *(1 Corinthians 15: 12)*.

The resurrection

Christians consider the resurrection of Jesus to be the strongest evidence of bodily resurrection. According to the Bible, the disciples saw, talked to, ate with and touched Jesus after his death: 'Look at my hands and my feet. It is I myself! Touch me and see; a ghost does not have flesh and bones, as you see I have' (*Luke 24: 39*). Christians believe the appearance of Jesus after the resurrection was not limited to the immediate disciples. Paul writes: 'After that he appeared to over 500 people, many of whom are still alive' *(1 Corinthians 15: 2)*.

STRETCH

Why do you think Paul makes a point of stating that many of the people who saw Jesus were still alive at the time of writing?

Christians believe that the resurrection of Jesus has made sure that there will be an afterlife for all who believe in him.

> ‘But because of his great love for us, God, who is rich in mercy, made us alive with Christ even when we were dead in transgressions—it is by grace you have been saved. **And God raised us up with Christ and seated us with him in the heavenly realms in Christ Jesus**, in order that in the coming ages he might show the incomparable riches of his grace, expressed in his kindness to us in Christ Jesus.’
> *(Ephesians 2: 4–7)*

A *The Resurrection* by Anton Laurids Johannes Dorph

This teaching supports the following Christian beliefs:

- Jesus' death and resurrection means that humanity can be saved (see 1.5)
- Jesus frees people from sin (transgressions) in an act of grace
- There is a place where God dwells ('the heavenly realms')
- Followers of Jesus are raised up to enjoy heaven with him.

Many Christians also believe that, at the end of time, God will raise their bodies to life again, as he did with Jesus' body (see 1.6).

What are other arguments for life after death?

Many religious and non-religious people believe in life after death. There are several key arguments to support this belief.

Remembered lives

Some people claim to be able to remember a past life, for example a child who is able to give details about a previous life that they couldn't have otherwise known anything about. Experiences like this are believed to support reincarnation – which means that a soul is born again in another body.

Reincarnation is not a Christian belief, and so most Christians would reject this as proof of the existence of life after death. Christians believe that each person has one life on Earth.

The paranormal

Some people, including **spiritualists**, believe that there is a spirit world beyond the physical one, where spirits of the dead live on and can be contacted through a medium – a person who has the ability to communicate with the dead. This is called belief in the **paranormal**.

People who believe in the paranormal may claim to have seen or experienced ghosts, visions of the dead, or telekinesis (objects moving without being touched). These people believe that such activities and experiences provide evidence for life after death.

> ‘The sacred gift of Spirit Communion was never meant to be used for entertainment, amusement or astonishment (*1 John 4: 1*), but rather for the comforting of the bereaved, the evolution of the soul, and the education, uplifting and spiritual advancement of humankind.’
> *(christianspiritualism.org)*

Spiritualist Church

B Many spiritualist churches draw inspiration from some Christian beliefs

Whilst Christians believe that there is an important, spiritual element to life, most Christians do not believe in the paranormal.

Logic

Some people would argue that it is logical to believe in life after death. They might argue that it seems logical that this life isn't all there is. They might also argue that near-death experiences can act as proof. This is when a person is medically understood to be dead for a short time and comes back to life, able to recall details such as approaching a bright light, or meeting with a religious figure.

Many Christians are wary about near-death experiences, and would argue that the evidence in the Bible is sufficient for a belief in the existence of life after death. Christians might argue that it

C

is logical to believe that there is an eternal life after death, based on arguments about the origins of the universe (see 4.1) – if an eternal God exists, and he is all loving, then people will join him when they die.

Reward

Some people believe that living a good life will mean that they will be rewarded somehow after they die. Christians believe in the Day of Judgement, when God will judge all people according to how they have lived their lives on Earth and to give them the afterlife they deserve (see 1.6). Non-religious people do not believe in God, but might believe that some system of justice or 'balance' will make sure that good people are rewarded.

Comfort

Some people believe that belief in life after death provides comfort for those who are suffering or who are mourning the loss of loved ones. Christians believe there is a better life to come and take comfort from this in difficult times.

Meeting loved ones

Some people believe that they will one day be able to meet loved ones who have already passed away. This belief is sometimes held because people sense their deceased loved ones are still with them – and therefore they believe they 'live on' in the afterlife.

Many Christians also believe that there will be the chance to meet loved ones who have passed away, but this belief is often based on Bible passages such as (*John 14: 1–3*) which describe being together with Jesus and other followers in heaven.

Why is belief in life after death significant for Christians?

- Christians believe life after death was a core reason why Jesus came to Earth – to free humanity from sin and enable them to live forever with God.
- Believing in life after death impacts a Christian's life: they believe that they will one day be with God in heaven, which gives them joy and hope for the future.
- Believing that God will one day judge people based on how they have lived their lives impacts the decisions that Christians make in their day-to-day lives.

SUMMARY

- Christian belief in the afterlife is very important, and is connected to beliefs about Jesus' own death and resurrection and what that means for Christians.
- Both religious and non-religious people can believe in life after death and will use a range of arguments to support their views.

USEFUL TERMS

Paranormal: experiences which suggest that there may be a non-visible, spirit world, such as ghosts and communications through mediums

Resurrection: rising from the dead; also the view that after death God recreates a new body in a heavenly place

Spiritualist: someone who believes that the spirits of dead people can communicate with living people

BUILD YOUR SKILLS

1 a Make a list of the arguments for life after death, and provide a short explanation for each one.
  b Which argument is the most convincing, and which is the least convincing? Write a paragraph explaining your views.

2 How can belief in life after death impact a person's life? Refer to Christian beliefs in your answer.

3 **STRETCH** Choose one of the following to research further: remembered lives, near-death experiences, telekinesis. How convincing are accounts of these? How would a Christian respond?

EXAM-STYLE QUESTIONS

a Outline **three** arguments for life after death. (3)

c Explain **two** reasons why Christians believe in the existence of life after death. In your answer you must refer to a source of wisdom and authority. (5)

4.6 Responses to arguments against life after death

SPECIFICATION FOCUS

Christian responses to non-religious arguments against life after death: why Christians reject arguments against belief in life after death (including as a source of comfort, lack of evidence, fraudulent accounts and social control), including 1 Peter 3: 18–22.

What are non-religious arguments against life after death, and how do Christians respond?

For most non-religious people there is no belief in an afterlife. Humanists suggest that Christians and other religious people spend too much time focusing on a 'life to come' and not enough time focusing on the one life they have:

> 'The more important question for [Humanists] is not whether there is an afterlife but how we should live this life [...] For humanists, the absence of an afterlife makes this life more important and meaningful than it would be if we had another life to live after it.'
> *(Humanist Perspectives: Death, British Humanist Association)*

Non-religious people put forward a wide range of reasons why they believe there is no life after death.

Source of comfort

Non-religious people may argue that the afterlife is merely a story made up to provide comfort to people who are bereaved (see case study below).

Christian responses

Christians do not believe the feeling of comfort, in itself, is proof of life after death. Christians base their beliefs on evidence from the Bible and find comfort in those beliefs. They disagree with the view that the afterlife is a made-up story – they strongly believe it is true.

A A 2009 atheist bus poster campaign

CASE STUDY: RICHARD DAWKINS

Richard Dawkins is a well-known biologist, author, and atheist, and argues against the existence of life after death:

> Wouldn't it be lovely to believe in an imaginary friend who listens to your thoughts, listens to your prayers, comforts you, consoles you, gives you life after death, can give you advice? Of course it's satisfying, if you can believe it. But who wants to believe a lie?
> *(Professor Richard Dawkins, 'The Problem with God' interview)*

B Richard Dawkins

SUPPORT What do you think about Dawkins' argument?

STRETCH Visit Dawkins' website. What are his beliefs and aims?

Lack of evidence

Many non-religious people believe that life after death is a belief which cannot be scientifically backed up by evidence. Beliefs about life after death are therefore seen to be wishful thinking.

Christian responses

A Christian could argue that science is not able to explain or prove everything, and certain beliefs require faith. Christians trust the evidence of the Bible and the resurrection of Jesus as arguments for the existence of life after death:

> ‘[You are saved] by the resurrection of Jesus Christ, who has gone into heaven and is at God's right hand...’
> *(1 Peter 3: 21–22)*

Fraudulent accounts

Humanists, atheists and some Christians comment that mediums and spiritualists who conduct séances, or sessions with individuals in which they apparently communicate with the spirits of the dead, may be simply exploiting those who are bereaved. Many mediums have been exposed as fraudulent, adding to the arguments of non-believers that there is no real evidence of the afterlife.

Christian responses

Most Christians would also be concerned that people who conduct séances, or sessions with individuals in which they apparently communicate with the spirits of the dead, might be exploiting those who are bereaved. An important principle in Christianity is integrity ('Speak the truth to each other', *Zechariah 8: 16*), and therefore Christians should not condone purposefully misleading people.

C Is there a difference between lighting a candle in church to remember a loved one who has passed away and going to a spiritualist church to try to speak to the deceased?

Social control

Beliefs in heaven and hell are central to several religions, and for many non-believers these are outdated and potentially damaging ideas. They argue that heaven and hell are ideas invented to control people's behaviour. In centuries past, it was common for Christian churches to teach believers about hell in order to frighten them into a certain way of behaving. This form of control by fear is often called social control. It would not be expected to happen in mainstream churches today, although some conservative church leaders may sometimes try to persuade people to become Christians by saying they will spend their afterlife in hell otherwise.

Christian responses

In response, Christians would say that just because some have used (and may continue to use) the threat of hell and/or the promise of heaven to control people, this does not mean that heaven and hell do not exist. They could argue that the practice of frightening people into becoming a Christian is not something Jesus would condone; his actions were intended to inspire people to love one another (*1 John 4: 7–12*). However, more conservative churches could argue that it is the loving thing to do to warn people about the possibility of hell.

BUILD YOUR SKILLS

1 Copy and complete the table below.

Reasons to reject belief in the afterlife	Christian responses	My observations

2 Consider what you have learned in 4.5 and 4.6.
   a Which is the most convincing argument for life after death (your answer to activity 1b in 4.5)?
   b Which is the most convincing argument against life after death?
   c Make a judgement: is there life after death? Write a conclusion and explain your reasons.

SUMMARY

- Many non-believers reject belief in an afterlife, because they believe there is no evidence for it, and argue that beliefs about the afterlife do not make sense.
- Others reject it because they see the idea of an afterlife as a way of controlling the behaviour and choices of believers.
- Christians would reject many of these arguments and offer alternative viewpoints about the existence of life after death.

EXAM-STYLE QUESTIONS

b Explain **two** reasons why a non-religious person would reject belief in life after death. (4)

d 'There is no good reason to believe in an afterlife.' Evaluate this statement considering arguments for and against. In your response you should:
- refer to Christian teachings
- refer to different Christian points of view
- refer to non-religious points of view
- reach a justified conclusion. (12)

4.7 Euthanasia

What is euthanasia?

Euthanasia is the deliberate administering of life-ending medication by a third party. Euthanasia is a Greek word which literally means 'good death'. It refers to the idea of 'easy death' or 'mercy killing'; that is, killing someone in order to end their pain and suffering. It is a very important issue in medical ethics today and although many people are against it, in some countries, such as the Netherlands, it is not against the law.

There are two types of euthanasia:

1. **Voluntary euthanasia** – a person's life is ended painlessly at their own request.
2. **Non-voluntary euthanasia** – a person's life is ended painlessly when they are unable to ask, but there are reasonable grounds for doing so (for example, a person cannot communicate but is in extreme pain).

Euthanasia can be active. This is a deliberate action performed by a third party to kill the person (for example, by lethal injection). Active euthanasia is illegal in the UK.

Doctors can also decide to withhold or withdraw medical treatment or life support that is keeping the person alive because they are not going to get better, or the person asks them to. Medical professionals call this a Non Treatment Decision. Controversially it is also sometimes called passive euthanasia.

Euthanasia should not be confused with assisted dying or assisted suicide. These involve the person themselves, and not a third party, completing the final action to end their own life. Assisted dying is when the person is terminally ill and dying, and assisted suicide is when the person is seriously ill but not dying.

SPECIFICATION FOCUS

Implications of Christian teachings about the value and sanctity of life for the issue of euthanasia: the nature of euthanasia; Christian teachings and divergent responses to euthanasia, including support for hospice care and interpretations of Job 2: 1–10; non-religious (including atheist and Humanist) arguments surrounding its use, including the application of ethical theories, such as situation ethics, and Christian responses to them.

USEFUL TERMS

Euthanasia: the deliberate administering of life-ending medication by a third party

Quality of life: the value given to life depending on how far a person can find enjoyment and pleasure from it

The case for euthanasia

Some people disagree with the law in the UK, and would argue that euthanasia should be made available. They could argue the following:

- Euthanasia allows the person to have a gentle, pain-free death and allows them to choose how and when they die.
- The patient dies with dignity, rather than slowly getting worse, mentally and physically.
- Euthanasia saves medical costs.
- Medics can focus their attention on patients who have a chance of recovery.
- It relieves the family of emotional and financial burdens.
- Euthanasia allows patients to decide when their **quality of life** is so low that they would prefer to die.

A Pro-euthanasia campaigners

The case against euthanasia

Some people are against euthanasia. These people could argue the following:

- Euthanasia requires a judgement to be made that a particular life is no longer worth living – but all people are valuable at all times.
- It might put pressure on sick people to choose euthanasia rather than seek a cure.
- Even if a sick person says they want to die, no one has the authority to take their life away.
- Doctors or relatives might make the choice without consulting the patient.
- No one can make a judgement about the value of another person's life.
- No person should value themselves as so worthless it would be better to die.
- Legalising even certain forms of euthanasia would be a 'slippery slope' – i.e. how can you be sure that voluntary euthanasia really is voluntary?

What do Christians believe about euthanasia?

As with abortion (see 4.4), many Christians object to euthanasia. For many Christians, including Catholics, Orthodox and many Protestants, it is wrong because:

- it goes against the principle of the sanctity of life
- taking away the life of a human being is murder, which is forbidden in the Bible
- God created human beings in his image so only he has the power to take away their lives
- terminally ill patients can still worship God and show other people God's love
- euthanasia could be used for evil purposes
- all people are equal in the sight of God, whatever their physical or mental condition, and all should be treated with dignity.

STRETCH

Find out about the work of Christian Action Research and Education (CARE) – a Christian organisation dedicated to promoting the sanctity of life.

Job

The Bible does not specifically mention euthanasia, however the closest it comes is in *Job 2: 9–10*. Job has a serious illness which has destroyed his quality of life, and his wife suggests voluntary suicide. Her intention is to end Job's pain by helping him to die.

> **'His wife said to him, 'Are you still maintaining your integrity? Curse God and die!' He replied, 'You are talking like a foolish woman. Shall we accept good from God, and not trouble?' In all this, Job did not sin in what he said.'**
> ***(Job 2: 9–10)***

Many Christians would argue that Job was being encouraged to euthanise himself, but he would not do so because it would be a sin if he did. Some Christians would disagree, however, and argue that Job had the potential to recover – and in fact, by the end of the book, his strength is fully restored.

The hospice movement

Many doctors argue that death need not be painful and undignified. The work of the **hospice** movement is dedicated to caring for terminally ill people by concentrating on pain relief. Advocates of the hospice movement could argue that euthanasia is an admission of defeat. However, hospice care can be expensive and is not always available.

B A hospice chapel

Respect and compassion

Many Christians believe that approaching death is a spiritual time because the dying person is getting closer to God and preparing for the afterlife. Respecting the dying person means:

- providing them with good-quality pain relief
- supporting them and those close to them as they prepare for death
- trusting the person's future to God.

Respecting the dying person may also include accepting their decision to cease having medical treatment that is prolonging their life. This is not the same as voluntary euthanasia, since it still allows God to make the decision about when they die.

SUPPORT Removing the medical treatment that is keeping a dying person alive allows the person to die naturally. Many Christians believe this is acceptable and is not euthanasia.

Supporting dying people is quite different from believing that people have the right to die. Most Christians believe that people do not have the right to end a life, and that it is therefore wrong to help someone to die, however ill they may be. These Christians believe that real compassion for someone in pain involves sharing that pain in a comforting way. However, not all Christians agree on this issue, and some Christians may still argue that euthanasia may be the most loving and kindest thing for people who are suffering.

What are some non-religious views about euthanasia?

Non-religious people might have a variety of views on euthanasia, for the reasons outlined on pages 130–131.

Humanists have supported attempts to legalise certain forms of euthanasia for many years (assisted suicide and voluntary euthanasia amongst them). Many non-religious people would be sympathetic to this position, but Humanists go a stage further:

> ‘We do not think that there is a strong moral case to limit assistance to terminally ill people alone and we wish to see reform of the law that would be responsive to the needs of other people who are permanently and incurably suffering.’
> *(British Humanist Association)*

C

In many ways the Humanist view of euthanasia is based on the principles of situation ethics (see 4.4): the idea of doing the most loving thing in any given situation. So if the most loving thing is to kill someone according to their wishes, then that is what should happen. However, a situation ethicist might also reach a different conclusion – they could argue that, in certain situations, the most loving thing to do would be to withhold euthanasia from someone who has requested it.

Most Christians would oppose the Humanist view that euthanasia should be made available to all people who are permanently suffering, arguing that all lives are valuable in the eyes of God, and suffering people can be cared for.

Some Christians would be sympathetic to the approach of situation ethicists, because they believe it is very important to show love to people. However, most Christians would not adopt this approach to decision-making. For example, Catholic Christians would instead abide by **Natural Law**, stated by Thomas Aquinas in the thirteenth century. Natural Law is a set of moral principles based on the idea that people should choose good actions that comply with God's wishes. At the heart of Natural Law is the idea that truth is universal and unchanging.

USEFUL TERMS

Hospice: a place which provides care for people with a serious, terminal, or incurable illness

Natural Law: a set of moral principles based on the idea that people should choose good actions that comply with God's wishes

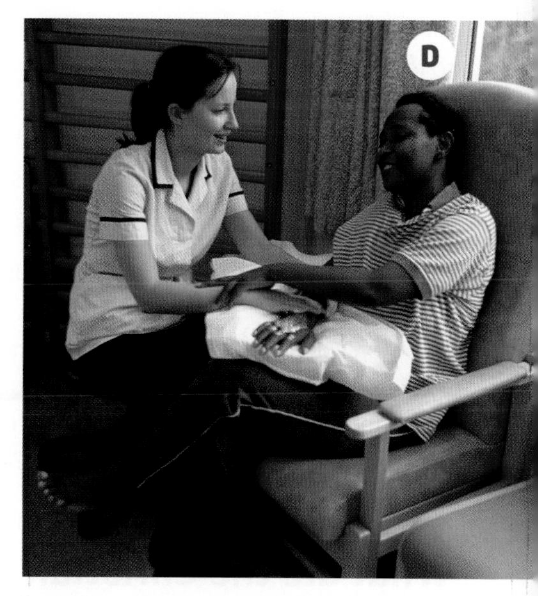
D

BUILD YOUR SKILLS

1. Create a mind map about euthanasia. Include on your mind map:
   - A definition of euthanasia, including different types and the UK law
   - Arguments for and against euthanasia, including Christian and non-religious viewpoints
   - Notes about how ethical theories can be applied to the issue.
2. Is there ever a time when a person's life is not worth living? Explain your views, referring to arguments for and against.

SUMMARY

- Euthanasia, providing a patient with an 'easy death' to avoid long-term pain, is illegal in the UK.
- There are different types of euthanasia. Many people campaign for voluntary euthanasia to be legalised.
- Arguments against euthanasia include the view that it undermines the value of all human life.
- Those in favour argue that people should be allowed to die how and when they wish.

EXAM-STYLE QUESTIONS

a. Outline **three** arguments in support of euthanasia. (3)

c. Explain **two** reasons why a Christian might oppose euthanasia. In your answer you must refer to a source of wisdom and authority. (5)

4.8 Issues in the natural world

SPECIFICATION FOCUS

Christian responses to issues in the natural world: Christian responses to threats to the world, including pollution, global warming and the use of natural resources; stewardship and humanity's role as stewards, including The Christian Declaration on Nature, Assisi 1986; differing Christian responses to animal rights, including animal experimentation and the use of animals for food, including the application of ethical theories such as utilitarianism.

What threats does the natural world face today?

The natural world faces many threats:

- pollution, including air, water and land pollution
- waste disposal
- global warming
- deforestation
- overuse of natural resources such as fuel and energy sources
- abuse of animals.

All these issues concern Christians who believe that humans have a responsibility to look after the world in which God has placed them. Fast-developing technology leads to a lot of waste which may not be recyclable or biodegradable. Waste takes up space and releases dangerous chemicals into the **environment**, but we are generating more of it, not less, every year.

Global temperatures have risen by 0.6°C in the past century. Shrinking ice caps, rising sea levels, and severe storms are all blamed on global warming.

> 'Man's dominion over inanimate and other living beings granted by the Creator is not absolute; it is limited by concern for the quality of life of his neighbour, including generations to come.'
> *(Catechism of the Catholic Church, 2415)*

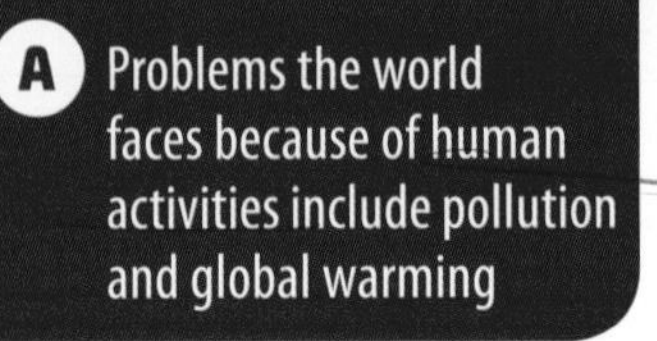

A Problems the world faces because of human activities include pollution and global warming

What are the Christian responses to these threats?

Dominion vs stewardship

Genesis 1: 28 states:

> 'God blessed them and said to them, 'Be fruitful and increase in number; fill the earth and subdue it. Rule over the fish in the sea and the birds in the sky and over every living creature that moves on the ground.''

The Old Testament was written in Hebrew. When it was being translated into English, various decisions were made around obscure words. One of those was the word that is translated here as 'rule', and as 'have dominion' in the King James Bible, which was translated nearly five centuries ago. These translations could give the idea of humanity being free to use Earth's resources for its own gains, without consideration of the damage. A better translation might have been 'steward', giving the idea that God was calling for humanity to be caretakers of the Earth. Only in recent history have people begun to understand humanity's responsibility to steward the Earth.

The Christian attitude to the environment is based on a perspective of **utilitarianism**; acting for the benefit of all, not just the present generations. There are three important concepts based on the belief that God created the natural world and gave it to humans to care for and protect:

- **stewardship** – care for the environment and its resources
- responsibility – it is up to humans to care for the natural world
- authority – the power to make a positive difference to the natural world.

USEFUL TERMS

Environment: the surroundings in which plants and animals live and on which they depend for life

Stewardship: looking after something so it can be passed on to the next generation

Utilitarianism: the belief that the right course of action is the one that will produce the greatest happiness of the greatest number of people

The Christian Declaration on Nature, Assisi 1986

In 1986, HRH Prince Philip, then President of the World Wildlife Fund, invited leaders of five world religions – Buddhism, Christianity, Hinduism, Islam, and Judaism – to meet to discuss how their faiths could help save the natural world. The meeting took place in Assisi in Italy, because it was the birthplace of St Francis, the Catholic saint of ecology. From this meeting arose key statements by the five faiths outlining their own distinctive traditions and approach to the care for nature. The statements became known as the Assisi Declarations on Nature.

CASE STUDY: THE CHRISTIAN DECLARATION ON NATURE

Therefore, in the name of Christ, who will come to judge the living and the dead, Christians repudiate:

- All forms of human activity – wars, discrimination, and destruction of cultures – which do not respect the authentic interests of the human race, in accordance with God's will and design, and do not enable men as individuals and as members of society to pursue and fulfil their total vocation within the harmony of the universe;
- All ill considered exploitation of nature which threatens to destroy it and, in turn, to make man the victim of degradation.

In the name of Christ, who will repay everyone for good works, Christians call upon all men and women to pursue:

- A synthesis between culture and faith;
- Ecumenical dialogue on the goals of scientific research and on the environmental consequences of the use of its findings;
- The priority of moral values over technological advances;
- Truth, justice and the peaceful coexistence of all peoples.

(Alliance of Religions and Conservation)

B HRH Prince Philip

❛If your religion tells you (as it does in Christianity anyway) that the Creation of the world was an act of God, then it follows naturally that if you belong to the church of God then you ought to look after His Creation [...] If we could get the local [religious] leaders to appreciate their responsibility for the environment then they would be able to explain that responsibility to the people of their faith.❜
(HRH Duke of Edinburgh, interview with Alliance of Religions and Conservation, 2003)

Care for animals

Many Christians believe that stewardship of the environment also involves stewardship of animals. This could include:

- campaigning against animal experimentation
- adopting vegetarian and vegan lifestyles
- protecting natural habitats
- supporting animals in their natural habitat
- conserving species
- banning animals in circuses and zoos
- challenging cruelty to animals.

However, some Christians believe that using animals for food and clothing, and experimentation on animals for medical research, are acceptable.

> 'God entrusted animals to the stewardship of those whom he created in his own image. Hence it is legitimate to use animals for food and clothing [...] Medical and scientific experimentation on animals is a morally acceptable practice if it remains within reasonable limits and contributes to caring for or saving human lives.'
> *(Catechism of the Catholic Church)*

Some Christian groups take an active stance on animal welfare issues. For example, the Anglican Society for the Welfare of Animals believes that humans have a duty to care for animals, and promotes reflection on the importance of animals through an annual Animal Welfare Sunday service, supports conservation activities, provides information about animal-related issues and campaigns over issues such as fox hunting.

> 'The Bible teaches us that God has given us 'dominion' not 'domination' over animals (*Genesis 1: 26*). This means 'loving care', not 'ruthless exploitation'.'
> *(Anglican Society for the Welfare of Animals website)*

C What do you think of the idea of Animal Sunday, when pets can be blessed in church? Not all Christians would agree with this practice.

The welfare of farmed animals is the focus of Creaturekind, an organisation that encourages Christians to explore 'how to put Christian faith into practice in all the ways we treat our fellow animal creatures'. They argue that 'new patterns of raising farmed animals are poor stewardship in ways that affect humans too, wasting scarce food and water supplies, causing environmental pollution, and contributing to climate change' (Creaturekind website).

D How do you think humans have contributed to each of the situations in these pictures? How does the concept of stewardship apply to these situations?

BUILD YOUR SKILLS

1 Why do Christians believe they should care for the natural world? Refer to stewardship, responsibility, and authority in your answer.

2 With a partner, try to put the Christian Declaration on Nature into your own words. In two different colours, underline:
   a the decisions that have been made
   b the core Christian beliefs that have been mentioned.

3 Do you think Christians should be for or against animal testing? Consider more than one viewpoint and give reasons.

4 Outline an argument that suggests utilitarianism is the most important Christian action.

STRETCH

SUMMARY

- Problems the world faces include pollution, global warming, waste, and exploitation of animals.
- Christian teaching on stewardship of the environment is based on Genesis where God gives humans responsibility to look after the natural world.
- Many Christians believe that animals should be treated with respect and care, but that it is acceptable to use them for human benefit up to a point. Some Christians disagree and oppose the use of animals for human benefit.

EXAM-STYLE QUESTIONS

a Outline **three** Christian responses to threats to the natural world. (3)

b Explain **two** different Christian beliefs about animal rights. (4)

Revision

BUILD YOUR SKILLS

Look at the list of 'I can' statements below and think carefully about how confident you are. Use the following code to rate each of the statements. Be honest!

Green – very confident. What is your evidence for this?

Orange – quite confident. What is your target? Be specific.

Red – not confident. What is your target? Be specific.

A self-assessment revision checklist is available on *Kerboodle*

I can...

- Give the scientific explanations for the origins of the universe
- Explain the Christian responses to these scientific explanations
- Explain why the universe is valuable according to Christian teaching
- Give some Christian responses to the idea that the universe can be used as a commodity, including a reference to a source of wisdom and authority
- Explain what 'sanctity of life' means and explain why Christians believe in it
- Give some Christian teachings about the sanctity of life, and explain what they mean
- Say why sanctity of life is important for Christians today
- Give the scientific and non-religious explanations for the origins of human life
- Give some Christian responses to these scientific explanations, and explain why these responses are significant for Christians today
- Give a definition of abortion
- Explain some different Christian responses to the issue of abortion, including pro-life and pro-choice arguments
- Explain how non-religious people might respond to the issue of abortion and how Christians might respond to them
- Explain how ethical theories could be applied to the issue of abortion and how a Christian might respond to them
- Explain Christian teachings and beliefs which support the existence of a life after death, with reference to a source of wisdom and authority
- Explain several different arguments (Christian and non-religious) for the existence of life after death
- Explain why belief in life after death is significant for Christians
- Explain some non-religious arguments against life after death
- Explain some reasons why Christians would reject non-religious arguments against life after death
- Give a definition of euthanasia
- Explain some different Christian responses to the issue of euthanasia, with reference to a source of wisdom and authority
- Explain how non-religious people might respond to the issue of euthanasia and how Christians might respond to them
- Explain how ethical theories could be applied to the issue of euthanasia and how a Christian might respond to them
- Describe some threats that are faced in the natural world today
- Explain some Christian responses to these threats
- Explain the different ways Christians respond to animal rights, including animal experimentation and the use of animals for food.

Exam practice

On these exam practice pages you will see example answers for each of the exam question types: **a**, **b**, **c**, and **d**. You can find out more about these on pages 6–11.

• Question 'a'

*Question **a** is AO1 – this tests your knowledge and understanding.*

(a) Outline **three** arguments for life after death. (3)

Student response

People argue for life after death if they have remembered something from before, or they want to be rewarded, or if they believe there is life after death.

WHAT WENT WELL

This student has touched on two arguments for life after death.

Improved student response

People argue for life after death if they have remembered something from a past life and believe they have been reincarnated, or if they believe in a system of justice where people will be rewarded in the life to come, or if they are a Christian and believe they will go to heaven to be with God.

HOW TO IMPROVE

A little more detail is required to ensure that the points are clear and accurate. Also, the student should take care to include three arguments for life after death – the last point is just a repeat of the question. See the 'improved student response' opposite for suggested corrections.

Over to you! Give yourself three minutes on the clock and have a go at answering this question. Remember, this question type requires you to provide three facts or short ideas: you don't need to explain them or express any opinions.

• Question 'b'

*Question **b** is AO1 – this tests your knowledge and understanding.*

(b) Explain **two** Christian teachings about the sanctity of life. (4)

Student response

The sanctity of life is the Christian teaching that all human life is holy. God planned each person before they even existed, therefore he knows all about them and cares about them.

WHAT WENT WELL

This student has correctly defined sanctity of life, and has provided another developed point about the sanctity of life.

Improved student response

The sanctity of life is the Christian teaching that all human life is holy. Christians believe human life is holy because God created human beings in his image and breathed life into them, passing on something of himself and his holiness to them.

Another Christian teaching is that God planned each person before they even existed, therefore he knows all about them and cares about them.

HOW TO IMPROVE

Whilst the definition of sanctity of life is correct, it is not a developed point. This student could also consider using a phrase to make it clear that they are providing two different Christian teachings. See the 'improved student response' opposite for suggested corrections.

Over to you! Give yourself four minutes on the clock and have a go at answering this question. Remember, in order to 'explain' something, you need to **develop** your points. See page 9 for a reminder of how to do this.

• Question 'c'

*Question **c** is AO1 – this tests your knowledge and understanding.*

(c) Explain **two** reasons why a Christian might oppose euthanasia. In your answer you must refer to a source of wisdom and authority. (5)

Student response

Many Christians would oppose euthanasia because they believe the Bible teaches against it (Job 2: 9–10).

Another reason is that euthanasia goes against the principle of the sanctity of life, because all human life is holy and valuable to God, and is therefore worth living even in difficult circumstances.

WHAT WENT WELL

This student has correctly identified two reasons why a Christian might oppose euthanasia, and has provided a reference to a source of wisdom and authority.

HOW TO IMPROVE

The first point is not explained. In 'c' questions you need to give two developed points **and** a reference to a source of wisdom and authority. See the 'improved student response' opposite for suggested corrections.

Improved student response

Many Christians would oppose euthanasia because they believe the Bible teaches against it. For example, in the story of Job, Job's decision not to die was said to be free from sin (Job 2: 9–10), and therefore Christians could conclude euthanasia to be a sinful act.

Another reason is that euthanasia goes against the principle of the sanctity of life, because all human life is holy and valuable to God, and is therefore worth living even in difficult circumstances.

Over to you! Give yourself five minutes on the clock and have a go at answering this question. Remember, you need to write two developed points, one of which needs to be supported by a source of wisdom and authority.

• Question 'd'

*Question **d** is AO2 – this tests your ability to evaluate.*

(d) 'Human life created itself.' Evaluate this statement considering arguments for and against. In your response you should:
- refer to Christian teachings
- refer to different Christian points of view
- refer to non-religious points of view
- reach a justified conclusion. (12)

Student response

This viewpoint relates to the issue of the origins of human life. The most widely held scientific viewpoint about the origins of human life is the theory of evolution by natural selection. This theory was first proposed by Charles Darwin in his book The Origin of Species *(1859). Non-religious people – including Humanists – would agree with the theory of evolution.*

Some Christians would reject scientific and non-religious explanations for the origins of human life because they believe that the creation of human life happened exactly as it is described in the Bible. Christians who read the creation story literally do not believe humans have evolved, because that's not how it is described in the Bible.

Other Christians believe that both the theory of evolution and the creation story in the Bible are true. These Christians do believe that God is personally involved in the process of evolution, which is something that non-religious people would disagree with.

In conclusion, I do agree with the viewpoint that human life made itself, because this is backed up by scientific evidence. However, the Christian argument that God made human life make itself is also convincing for those who believe in God.

WHAT WENT WELL

The student refers to the statement in the question, describes two different Christian points of view, and reaches a justified conclusion.

HOW TO IMPROVE

The student has referred to non-religious points of view, but has not explained them. Some detail about the theory of evolution would improve this answer. A better answer would also need to include relevant sources of wisdom and authority. Have a look at this improved version of the student response.

Improved student response

This viewpoint relates to the issue of the origins of human life. The most widely held scientific viewpoint about the origins of human life is the theory of evolution by natural selection. This theory was first proposed by Charles Darwin in his book The Origin of Species (1859).

Non-religious people – including Humanists – would agree with the view of scientists that human life evolved over a long period of time (sharing a common ancestry with apes) because of a principle called survival of the fittest. This means that individuals who have features that are best suited to their environment are the most likely to survive and pass on their genes. These features are passed on to the next generation, and so on. Scientific evidence backs up this theory.

Some Christians would reject scientific and non-religious explanations for the origins of human life because they believe that the creation of human life happened exactly as it is described in the Bible. Christians who read the creation story literally do not believe humans have evolved, because the Bible says God created man from 'the dust in the ground' (Genesis 2: 7). Young Earth Creationists believe the universe is around 10,000 years old, which contradicts the far greater timescale given to the process of evolution.

Other Christians believe that both the theory of evolution and the creation story in the Bible are true. In 2010 the General Synod of the Church of England concluded that mainstream science and Christian thought were compatible, because Genesis is a metaphorical account. These Christians do believe that God is personally involved in the process of evolution, which is something that non-religious people would disagree with.

In conclusion, I do agree with the viewpoint that human life made itself, because this is backed up by scientific evidence. However, the Christian argument that God made human life make itself is also convincing for those who believe in God.

Over to you! Give yourself 12 minutes on the clock and have a go at answering this question. Remember to refer back to the original statement in your writing when you give different points of view, and make sure you cover each of the bullet points given in the question.

BUILD YOUR SKILLS

In your exams, you'll need to make sure you use religious terminology correctly. Do you know the meaning of the following important terms for this topic?

- commodity
- sanctity of life
- survival of the fittest
- abortion
- situation ethics
- paranormal
- euthanasia
- hospice
- stewardship

Glossary

39 Articles of Religion a historical record of beliefs (or 'doctrines') held by the Church of England

abortion ending a pregnancy by deliberately removing a foetus by surgical or medical means

abstinence choosing to restrain oneself from doing something, for example, having sex or eating food (also called fasting)

adultery when a married person has a sexual relationship with someone other than their spouse

Advent a season of preparation for Christmas

Alpha a course run by churches and local Christian groups which enables people to find out more about the Christian faith in a relaxed setting

annulment declaration that a marriage is null and void; in effect, as if it had never happened, for reasons such as being under age or being forced to marry

anoint apply oil to a person's head as a sign of holiness and God's approval

ascension going up into heaven

atheist someone who does not believe in the existence of God

atonement the action of restoring a relationship; in Christianity, Jesus' death and resurrection restores the relationship between God and human beings

baptism the Christian ceremony that welcomes a person into the Christian community

begotten born of

benevolence all-good

Big Bang Theory a scientific theory about the origin of the universe which suggests that the universe is expanding away from a single point, a process which started around 13.7 billion years ago

charismatic a power given by God, e.g. inspired teaching

charity giving to those in need

Christingle a lighted candle symbolising Jesus as the light of the world; often carried by children in church celebrations around Christmas time

cohabitation living together in a sexual relationship but without legalising the union through marriage

commodity a useful or valuable thing which satisfies particular wants or needs

conception the moment when a sperm fertilises an egg, creating an embryo that can develop into a baby

conservation protecting something from being damaged or destroyed

contraception artificial and natural methods of preventing pregnancy; also known as birth control

convert to change from one set of beliefs to another

creationism the belief that the world was created in a literal six days and that Genesis is a scientific/historical account of the beginning of the world

creed a statement of firmly held beliefs; for example, the Apostles' Creed or the Nicene Creed

crucifixion being nailed to a cross and left to die

Day of Judgement God assesses a person's life and actions

denominations the name given to the main groups within the Church

divorce the legal ending of a marriage

ecumenism a movement that tries to bring different Christian denominations closer together

environment the surroundings in which plants and animals live and on which they depend for life

epiphany a moment of suddenly revealing something surprising or great

equality treating people in the same way irrespective of differences such as sex, race, education, disability or sexuality

eschatology an area of Christian theology which is concerned with life after death

Eucharist the ceremony commemorating the Last Supper, involving bread and wine; also called Holy Communion or Mass

euthanasia the deliberate administering of life-ending medication by a third party

evangelism preaching the gospel in order to attract new believers

evolution the process by which different species have developed from earlier forms

faithfulness not having a sexual relationship with anyone other than a partner

free will having the freedom to choose what to do

Gay Pride see **Pride**

gender discrimination acting upon prejudice about someone's gender; for example, not appointing a woman to a high-pressure job on the assumption that she must be too fragile for the role; or expecting a man to do a heavy physical task on the assumption that he must be strong

gender prejudice making judgements about men or women on the basis of their gender; for example, judging all women to be emotionally fragile or all men to be emotionally strong

General Synod the national group within the Church of England that debates issues relating to Christian belief and practice

grace undeserved love

heaven place of eternal paradise where Christians believe they will spend the afterlife

hell place of punishment and separation from God

heterosexuality sexual attraction to members of the opposite sex

Holy Spirit the Spirit of God, who gives the power to understand and worship

Holy Week the week before Easter

homosexuality sexual attraction to members of the same sex

hospice a place which provides care for people with a serious, terminal, or incurable illness

Humanist a non-religious person who looks to reason and empathy in order to live a meaningful life

humanity all human beings

immortal soul a soul that lives on after the death of the physical body

incarnation to take on flesh; God becomes a human being

intercession prayers for those who are suffering

Jesus Christ the Son of God, who came into the world as a human being

law guidelines as to how people should behave

liturgical a set form of worship, usually following agreed words

local church a meeting place for local believers and the community of believers who gather there

marriage the legal union of a man and a woman or a same-sex couple

mission sending individuals or groups to spread the Christian message

missionary a person who preaches and invites people to convert to the Christian faith

moral evil suffering caused by humans, such as war

nativity the birth of someone

natural evil suffering caused by natural events, such as earthquakes

Natural Law a set of moral principles based on the idea that people should choose to do good actions that comply with God's wishes

non-liturgical a form of worship which is not set

omnipotence all-powerful

ordination the appointment of men and women to professional ministry in the Church

outreach an activity to provide services to people in need

paranormal experiences which suggest that there may be a non-visible, spirit world, such as ghosts or communications through mediums

parish a community of local believers within a particular denomination

Pentecostalism a Protestant movement that puts special emphasis on a direct and personal relationship with God through the Holy Spirit

persecution the ill-treatment of an individual or group, usually on the grounds of religion, politics or ethnicity

pilgrimage a journey to a religious or holy place

prayer a way of communicating with God

Pride or **Gay Pride** a social movement encouraging homosexual people to express their sexuality openly and with self-esteem

pro-choice holding the belief that the mother should be able to choose whether to have an abortion

pro-life holding the belief that the foetus has a right to life

procreation to have sex and produce children

promiscuity sexual relations with multiple partners on a casual basis

prophecy a message from God in which he communicates his will

purgatory a place where the souls of the dead are cleansed and prepared for heaven

quality of life the value given to life depending on how far a person can find enjoyment and pleasure from it

reconciliation restoring peace and friendship between individuals or groups

repentance to say sorry for, and turn away from, any wrongdoing

resurrection rising from the dead; also the view that after death God recreates a new body in a heavenly place

rites of passage events marking key stages in life

sacrament an important Christian ceremony

salvation being saved from sin and the consequences of sin; going to heaven

sanctity of life the belief that life is created by God and made holy by him

sanctity of marriage the idea that marriage has special significance as a holy gift from God

Satan 'the adversary'; one of God's angels who rebelled against the rule of God

sermon a talk or teaching from a church leader

shrine a holy place

sin anything that prevents a relationship with God, either because the person does something they shouldn't, or neglects to do something they should

situation ethics ethical decisions made according to the specific context of the decision

spiritual gifts gifts given by God to believers, e.g. speaking in 'tongues', a special language

spiritualist someone who believes that the spirits of dead people can communicate with living people

stewardship looking after something so it can be passed on to the next generation

survival of the fittest the idea that members of a species that are best suited to an environment survive

Trinity God as one being, in three persons

universalism the belief that because of the love and mercy of God everyone will go to heaven

utilitarianism the belief that the right course of action is the one that will produce the greatest happiness of the greatest number of people

vale of soul-making an environment in which human beings can overcome evil by making good choices

vigil staying awake at night in order to pray; also the name given to the celebration of a festival on the eve before the festival itself

vision seeing or hearing someone or something holy

worship believers expressing love and respect for, and devotion to, God

Index

M

N

O

P

Q

R

S

T

U

V

W

Acknowledgements

We are grateful to the authors and publishers for use of extracts from their titles and in particular for the following:

Scripture quotations taken from the **Holy Bible, New International Version Anglicised** Copyright © 1979, 1984, 2011 Biblica. Used by permission of Hodder & Stoughton Ltd, an Hachette UK company. All rights reserved. 'NIV' is a registered trademark of Biblica UK trademark number 1448790.

Excerpts from **Book of Common Prayer**, the rights in which are vested in the Crown, are reproduced by permission of the Crown's Patentee, Cambridge University Press https://www.churchofengland.org/prayer-worship/worship/book-of-common-prayer/articles-of-religion.aspx (Cambridge University Press, 2004). Reproduced with permission from Cambridge University Press.

Excerpts from **Catechism of the Catholic Church**, http://www.vatican.va/archive/ccc_css/archive/catechism/ccc_toc.htm (Strathfield, NSW: St Pauls, 2000). © Libreria Editrice Vaticana. Reproduced with permission from The Vatican.

Action for Children: Our Methodist Partnership, https://www.actionforchildren.org.uk/who-we-are/our-methodist-partnership/ (Action for Children, 2016). Reproduced with permission from Action for Children www.actionforchildren.org.uk

Alliance of Religions and Conservation: Assisi Declarations on Nature, http://www.arcworld.org/faiths.asp?pageID=179 (ARC, 1986). Reproduced with permission from Alliance of Religions and Conservation.

Alliance of Religions and Conservation: Duke of Edinburgh Interview with Alliance of Religions and Conservation, http://www.arcworld.org/news.asp?pageID=1 (ARC, 2003). Reproduced with permission from Alliance of Religions and Conservation.

T. Bisson: quote, http://christianspiritualism.org (ChristianSpiritualism.org, 2016). Reproduced with permission from T. Bisson, owner of christianspiritualism.org.

Children's Society: About Us, www.childrenssociety.org.uk (Children's Society, 2016). Reproduced with permission from The Children's Society.

Christian Aid: About Us, http://www.christianaid.org.uk/aboutus/who/aims/our_aims.aspx (Christian Aid, 2016). Reproduced with permission from Christian Aid

The Church of England: Abortion, https://www.churchofengland.org/our-views/medical-ethics-health-social-care-policy/abortion.aspx (The Church of England, 2016). © The Archbishops' Council of the Church of England. Reproduced with permission from The Archbishops' Council.

The Church of England: Abortion, https://www.churchofengland.org/media/45673/abortion.pdf (The Church of England, 2005). © The Archbishops' Council of the Church of England. Reproduced with permission from The Archbishops' Council.

The Church of England: Common Worship, (Church of England, 2016). © The Archbishops' Council of the Church of England. Reproduced with permission from The Archbishops' Council.

The Church of England: Domestic Abuse: Guidelines for Those with Pastoral Responsibilities, (The Church of England, 2006). © The Archbishops' Council of the Church of England. Reproduced with permission from The Archbishops' Council.

The Church of England: Family, www.churchofengland.org/our-views/marriage,-family-and-sexuality-issues/family.aspx (The Church of England, 2016). © The Archbishops' Council of the Church of England. Reproduced with permission from The Archbishops' Council.

The Church of England: Homosexual Relationships: A Contribution to Discussion by Church of England Board for Social Responsibility, (Church of England Board for Social Responsibility, 1979). © The Archbishops' Council of the Church of England. Reproduced with permission from The Archbishops' Council.

The Church of England: Statement on Marriage, (The Church of England, 2016). © The Archbishops' Council of the Church of England. Reproduced with permission from The Archbishops' Council.

Creature Kind: About Us, www.becreaturekind.org, (Be Creature Kind, 2016). Reproduced with permission from Creature Kind | BeCreatureKind.org

R. Dawkins: The Problem with God: Interview with Richard Dawkins, http://www.beliefnet.com/news/science-religion/2005/11/the-problem-with-god-interview-with-richard-dawkins.aspx? (Beliefnet, 2016). Reproduced with permission from R. Dawkins.

P. Jenkins: Changing Family Structures in Church Life, March/April 2016, https://www.evangelicalmagazine.com/article/changing-family-structures-in-church-life/ (Bryntirion Press, 2016). Reproduced with permission from Bryntirion Press.

G. Kendrick: Shine, Jesus, Shine, (Make Way Music, 1987) Graham Kendrick © (1987) Make Way Music. www.grahamkendrick.co.uk. Reproduced with permission from Make Way Music.

G. Lemaître: Life, Science and Legacy, edited by Rodney D. Holder and Simon Mitton, (Springer, 2013). Reproduced with permission from Springer.

The Methodist Church in Britain: Abortion, http://www.methodist.org.uk/downloads/coun-1004-abortion-190110.pdf (The Methodist Church, 2009). © Trustees for Methodist Church Purposes. Reproduced with permission from The Methodist Church in Britain.

The Methodist Church in Britain: Domestic Abuse, (The Methodist Church, 2005). Copyright holder not established at time of going to print. © Trustees for Methodist Church Purposes. Reproduced with permission from The Methodist Church in Britain.We have made every effort to trace and contact all copyright holders before publication, but if notified of any errors or omissions, the publisher will be happy to rectify these at the earliest opportunity.

The publisher would like to thank the following for permission to use their photographs:

COVER: Digital Vision/Getty Images

contents/revision page backgrounds: mironov/Shutterstock; **p4**: Lolostock / Shutterstock; **p6**: Photoonlife / Shutterstock; **p7**: totallypic / Shutterstock; **p8**: Nikolaeva / Shutterstock; **p9**: SH-Vector / Shutterstock; **p11**: Sutichak / Shutterstock; **p10**: Tang Yan Song / Shutterstock; **p12**: mangostock / Shutterstock; **p13**: Art Directors & TRIP / Alamy Stock Photo; **p14**: Photobank gallery/Shutterstock; **p14**: Eugene Sergeev/Shutterstock; **p17**: The Baptism of Christ, c.1580-88 (oil on canvas), Veronese, (Paolo Caliari) (1528-88) / © Samuel Courtauld Trust, The Courtauld Gallery, London, UK / Bridgeman Images; **p18**: © Jeff Gilbert / Alamy Stock Photo; **p19**: Lisa S./Shutterstock; **p21**:

robert_s/Shutterstock; **p22**: © Gregg Vignal / Alamy Stock Photo; **p23**: Amy Watts; **p24**: © AF archive / Alamy Stock Photo; **p25**: © Paul Rapson / Alamy Stock Photo; **p26**: © Archivart / Alamy Stock Photo; **p27**: Photobank gallery/Shutterstock; **p28**: © AF archive / Alamy Stock Photo; **p28**: Lokibaho/iStock; **p29**: Colin Underhill / Alamy Stock Photo; **p30**: Heritage Image Partnership Ltd / Alamy Stock Photo; **p31**: © Archivart / Alamy Stock Photo; **p32**: Samuel Cohen / Shutterstock; **p33**: Iakov Kalinin/Shutterstock; **p34**: Iulian Dragomir/Shutterstock; **p34**: Steve Skjold/Alamy Stock Photo; **p36**: WitthayaP/Shutterstock; **p36**: ZUMA Press, Inc. / Alamy Stock Photo; **p38**: Jorge Fajl/National Geographic Creative/Corbis; **p39**: Eugene Sergeev/Shutterstock; **p40**: © Design Pics Inc / Alamy Stock Photo; **p41**: Michaelpuche/ Shutterstock; **p46**: Adrian Buck / Alamy Stock Photo; **p46**: Jim Ritchie / Alamy Stock Photo; **p48**: dominic dibbs / Alamy Stock Photo; **p49**: Adrian Buck / Alamy Stock Photo; **p50**: Patrick Ward / Alamy Stock Photo; **p51**: Jim Ritchie / Alamy Stock Photo; **p53**: Jack Frog / Shutterstock; **p54**: Funcrunch Photo / Alamy Stock Photo; **p54**: Lesbian and Gay Christian Movement / www.lgcm.org.uk; **p55**: dbimages / Alamy Stock Photo; **p57**: MBI / Alamy Stock Photo; **p57**: DGLimages / Shutterstock; **p58**: The Children's Society / www.childrenssociety.org.uk; **p59**: Richard Donovan / Alamy Stock Photo; **p60**: St Michael's Church, Warfield; **p60**: Antonio Gravante / Shutterstock; **p63**: Tony Smith / Alamy Stock Photo; **p63**: Phanie / Alamy Stock Photo; **p64**: aerogondo2 / shutterstock; **p65**: Glasshouse Images / Alamy Stock Photo; **p65**: epa european pressphoto agency b.v. / Alamy Stock Photo; **p66**: Sam72 / Shutterstock; **p67**: Francisco Martinez / Alamy Stock Photo; **p68**: Godong / Alamy Stock Photo; **p69**: michaeljung / Shutterstock; **p71**: Gruffydd Thomas / Alamy Stock Photo; **p72**: Cultura RM / Alamy Stock Photo; **p73**: Mike Goldwater / Alamy Stock Photo; **p73**: epa european pressphoto agency b.v. / Alamy Stock Photo; **p73**: epa european pressphoto agency b.v. / Alamy Stock Photo; **p73**: epa european pressphoto agency b.v. / Alamy Stock Photo; **p76**: Skim New Media Limited / Alamy Stock Photo; **p76**: Nancy Bauer / Shutterstock; **p78**: Pontino / Alamy Stock Photo; **p79**: Art Directors & TRIP / Alamy Stock Photo; **p81**: Thoom / Shutterstock; **p82**: TerryHealy / Getty Images; **p83**: Mkucova / iStock; **p84**: Godong / Alamy Stock Photo; **p85**: Chokniti Khongchum / Shutterstock; **p86**: elenaleonova / Getty Images; **p86**: Granger, NYC. / Alamy Stock Photo; **p87**: Mary Evans Picture Library / Alamy Stock Photo; **p88**: Muammar Awad/Anadolu Agency/Getty Images; **p89**: robertharding / Alamy Stock Photo; **p90**: Barry Lewis / Alamy Stock Photo; **p91**: KAREN MINASYAN/AFP/Getty Images; **p92**: The Resurrection of Christ and the Pious Women at the Sepulchre, 1442 (fresco), Angelico, Fra (Guido di Pietro) (c.1387-1455) / Museo di San Marco dell'Angelico, Florence, Italy / Bridgeman Images; **p93**: Amy Mikler / Alamy Stock Photo; **p94**: Borderlands / Alamy Stock Photo; **p95**: Alpha; **p97**: Peter Noyce GEN / Alamy Stock Photo; **p97**: Jim West / Alamy Stock Photo; **p98**: Vatican Pool/Getty Images; **p99**: epa european pressphoto agency b.v. / Alamy Stock Photo; **p101**: Rana Sajid Hussain/Pacific Press/LightRocket via Getty Images; **p101**: Frances Roberts / Alamy Stock Photo; **p102**: Sam Spickett / Christian Aid; **p110**: B Christopher / Alamy; **p110**: Adam Radosavljevic / Shutterstock; **p112**: age fotostock / Alamy Stock Photo; **p113**: GL Archive / Alamy Stock Photo; **p114**: Mark Henderson / Alamy Stock Photo; **p114**: Barry Diomede / Alamy Stock Photo; **p115**: Smit / Shutterstock; **p116**: EdBockStock / Alamy Stock Photo; **p117**: Classic Image / Alamy Stock Photo; **p117**: LIONEL BRET/LOOK AT SCIENCES/SCIENCE PHOTO LIBRARY; **p119**: Jeff Morgan 11 / Alamy Stock Photo; **p120**: Gulei Ivan / Shutterstock EDELMANN/SCIENCE PHOTO LIBRARY; **p120**: Yulia Sribna / Shutterstock; **p122**: Keystone Pictures USA / Alamy Stock Photo; **p122**: Jim West / Alamy Stock Photo; **p122**: B Christopher / Alamy Stock Photo; **p124**: SuperStock / Getty Images; **p125**: Keystone Pictures USA / Alamy Stock Photo; **p125**: Adam Radosavljevic / Shutterstock; **p127**: Jeff Morgan 07 / Alamy Stock Photo; **p127**: Jenny Matthews / Alamy Stock Photo; **p128**: Frank Gaertner / Shutterstock; **p128**: Photographee.eu / Shutterstock; **p130**: Janine Wiedel Photolibrary / Alamy Stock Photo; **p132**: John Robertson / Alamy Stock Photo; **p132**: Agencja Fotograficzna Caro / Alamy Stock Photo; **p133**: BH Generic Stock Images / Alamy Stock Photo; **p134**: PhotoAlto / Alamy Stock Photo; **p134**: MJ Photography / Alamy Stock Photo; **p135**: epa european pressphoto agency b.v. / Alamy Stock Photo; **p136**: jacky chapman / Alamy Stock Photo; **p137**: Cristina Simon / Shutterstock; **p137**: Nature Picture Library / Alamy Stock Photo; **p137**: incamerastock / Alamy Stock Photo